CONFEDERATION OF TOURISM AND HOSPITALITY

The Tourism Industry

Study Guide

THIS STUDY GUIDE

BPP Learning Media is the **official publisher** for the CTH Diplomas in Hotel Management and Tourism Management.

IN THIS JULY 2009 FIRST EDITION

- The CTH 2009 syllabus, cross-referenced to the chapters
- Comprehensive syllabus coverage, reviewed and approved by CTH
- Plenty of activities, examples and discussion topics to demonstrate and practise technique
- Full index
- A full CTH past exam for exam practice

First edition July 2009

ISBN 9780 7517 7794 9

British Library Cataloguing-in-Publication Data
A catalogue record for this book
is available from the British Library

Published by

BPP Learning Media Ltd
BPP House, Aldine Place
London W12 8AA

www.bpp.com/learningmedia

Printed in the United Kingdom

Your learning materials, published by BPP Learning
Media Ltd, are printed on paper sourced from
sustainable, managed forests.

We are grateful to the Confederation of Tourism and
Hospitality for permission to reproduce the syllabus and
past examination questions and answers.

©
BPP Learning Media
2009

CONTENTS

How to use this Study Guide

This is the first edition of BPP Learning Media's ground-breaking Study Guide for the *Tourism Industry* paper of the CTH Diplomas in Hotel and Tourism Management. It has been specifically written to cover the syllabus, and has been fully reviewed by CTH.

To pass the examination you need a thorough understanding in all areas covered by the syllabus.

Recommended approach

(a) To pass you need to be able to answer questions on **everything** specified by the syllabus. Read the Study Guide very carefully and do not skip any of it.

(b) Learning is an **active** process. Do **all** the activities as you work through the Study Guide so you can be sure you really understand what you have read.

(c) After you have covered the material in the Study Guide, work through the questions in the practice exam at the back.

(d) Before you take the real exam, check that you still remember the material using the following quick revision plan.

   (i) Read through the chapter learning objectives. Are there any gaps in your knowledge? If so, study the section again.

   (ii) Read and learn the key terms.

   (iii) Read and try to memorise the summary at the end of each chapter.

   (iv) Do the self-test questions again. If you know what you're doing, they shouldn't take long.

This approach is only a suggestion. You or your college may well adapt it to suit your needs.

Remember this is a **practical** course.

(a) Try to relate the material to your experience in the workplace or any other work experience you may have had.

(b) Try to make as many links as you can to other CTH papers that you may be studying at the moment.

Help yourself study for your CTH exams

Exams for professional bodies such as CTH are very different from those you may have taken at school or college. You will be under **greater time pressure** before the exam – as you may be combining your study with work. There are many different ways of learning and so the BPP Learning Media Study Guide offers you a number of different tools to help you through. Here are some hints and tips: they are not plucked out of the air, but **based on research and experience**. (You don't need to know that long-term memory is in the same part of the brain as emotions and feelings – but it's a fact anyway.)

The right approach

1   **The right attitude**

> **Believe in yourself**
>
> Yes, there is a lot to learn. Yes, it is a challenge. But thousands have succeeded before and you can too.
>
> **Remember why you're doing it**
>
> Studying might seem a grind at times, but you are doing it for a reason: to advance your career.

2   **The right focus**

Read through the syllabus and the chapter objectives

These tell you what you are expected to know.

Study the Exam Paper section

It helps to be familiar with the structure of the exam that you are going to take.

3   **The right method**

The whole picture

You need to grasp the detail – but keeping in mind how everything fits into the whole picture will help you understand better.

- The **objectives and topic list** of each chapter put the material in context.
- The **syllabus content** shows you what you need to **grasp**.

In your own words

To absorb the information (and to practise your written communication skills), it helps to **put it into your own words**.

- **Take notes**.
- Answer the **questions** in each chapter. You will practise your written communication skills, which become increasingly important as you progress through your CTH exams.
- Draw **mindmaps**. The chapter summaries can be a good starting point for this.
- Try **'teaching' a subject** to a colleague or friend.

Give yourself cues to jog your memory

The BPP Study Guide uses **bold** to **highlight key points**.

- Try **colour coding** with a highlighter pen.
- Write **key points** on cards.

4   **The right review**

Review, review, review

It is a **fact** that regularly reviewing a topic in summary form can **fix it in your memory**. Because **review** is so important, the BPP Study Guide helps you to do so in many ways.

- **Chapter summaries** draw together the key points in each chapter. Use them to recap each study session.
- The **self-test questions** are another review technique you can use to ensure that you have grasped the essentials.
- Go through the **examples and illustrations** in each chapter a second or third time.

Developing your personal study plan

BPP's **Learning to Learn Accountancy** book (which can be successfully used by students studying for any professional qualification) emphasises the need to prepare (and use) a study plan. Planning and sticking to the plan are key elements of learning success.

There are four steps you should work through.

STEP 1   **How do you learn?**

First you need to be aware of your style of learning. The BPP Learning Media **Learning to Learn Accountancy** book commits a chapter to this **self-discovery**. What types of intelligence do you display when learning? You might be advised to brush up on certain study skills before launching into this Study Guide.

BPP Learning Media's **Learning to Learn Accountancy** book helps you to identify what intelligences you show more strongly and then details how you can tailor your study process to your preferences. It also includes handy hints on how to develop intelligences you exhibit less strongly, but which might be needed as you study for your professional qualification.

Are you a **theorist** or are you more **practical**? If you would rather get to grips with a theory before trying to apply it in practice, you should follow the study sequence on page (vii). If the reverse is true (you like to know why you are learning theory before you do so), you might be advised to flick through Study Guide chapters and look at examples, case studies and questions (Steps 8, 9 and 10 in the **suggested study sequence**) before reading through the detailed theory.

STEP 2   **How much time do you have?**

Work out the time you have available per week, given the following.

- The standard you have set yourself
- The time you need to set aside later for revision work
- The other exam(s) you are sitting
- Very importantly, practical matters such as work, travel, exercise, sleep and social life

Hours

Note your time available each week in box A.   A   [   ]

STEP 3   **Allocate your time**

- Take the time you have available per week for this Study Guide shown in box A, multiply it by the number of weeks available and insert the result in box B.   B   [   ]

- Divide the figure in box B by the number of chapters in this text and insert the result in box C.   C   [   ]

Remember that this is only a rough guide. Some of the chapters in this book are longer and more complicated than others, and you will find some subjects easier to understand than others.

STEP 4   **Implement**

Set about studying each chapter in the time shown in box C, following the key study steps in the order suggested by your particular learning style.

This is your personal **study plan**. You should try and combine it with the study sequence outlined below. You may want to modify the sequence a little (as has been suggested above) to adapt it to your **personal style**.

BPP Learning Media's **Learning to Learn Accountancy** gives further guidance on developing a study plan, and deciding where and when to study.

BPP LEARNING MEDIA

Suggested study sequence

It is likely that the best way to approach this Study Guide is to tackle the chapters in the order in which you find them. Taking into account your individual learning style, you could follow this sequence.

Key study steps	Activity
Step 1 **Topic list**	Look at the topic list at the start of each chapter. Each topic represents a section in the chapter.
Step 2 **Explanations**	Proceed methodically through the chapter, reading each section thoroughly and making sure you understand.
Step 3 **Definitions**	Definitions can often earn you **easy marks** if you state them clearly and correctly in an appropriate exam answer
Step 4 **Note taking**	Take brief notes, if you wish. Avoid the temptation to copy out too much. Remember that being able to put something into your own words is a sign of being able to understand it. If you find you cannot explain something you have read, read it again before you make the notes.
Step 5 **Examples**	Follow each through to its solution very carefully.
Step 6 **Discussion topics**	Study each one, and try to add flesh to them from your own experience. They are designed to show how the topics you are studying come alive (and often come unstuck) in the real world.
Step 7 **Activities**	Make a very good attempt at each one.
Step 8 **Answers**	Check yours against ours, and make sure you understand any discrepancies.
Step 9 **Chapter summary**	Work through it carefully, to make sure you have grasped the significance of all the key areas.
Step 10 **Self-test questions**	When you are happy that you have covered the chapter, use the self-test questions to check how much you have remembered of the topics covered and to practise questions in a variety of formats.
Step 11 **Question practice**	Either at this point, or later when you are thinking about revising, make a full attempt at the practice exam.

Moving on...

However you study, when you are ready to start your revision, you should still refer back to this Study Guide, both as a source of **reference** (you should find the index particularly helpful for this) and as a way to **review** (the chapter summaries and self-test questions help you here).

And remember to keep careful hold of this Study Guide – you will find it invaluable in your work.

> More advice on study skills can be found in BPP Learning Media's **Learning to Learn Accountancy book**.

Syllabus

DIPLOMA PROGRAMMES MODULE SYLLABUS

DHM 172: The Tourism Industry
DTM 112: The Tourism Industry

Description

The aim of this module is to provide students with a broad introduction to the world of tourism. It provides an overview of the nature of tourism and tourism products from both local and international perspectives. It will ensure students acquire an understanding of the travel and tourism industry, including the impacts of tourism on destination economies, environments and cultures.

Summary of learning outcomes

On completion of this module students will be able to:

- Demonstrate knowledge of the travel and tourism industry

- Describe the structure of the tourism industry

- Examine the role of governments, political issues and ethics on tourism

- Analyse a range of tourist needs and motivations to travel

- Understand the development of tourism destinations

- Explain the range of transport and accommodation available

- Appraise the positive and negative impacts of economic, environmental and socio-cultural tourism

Syllabus		Chapter
Introduction to the travel and tourism industry	The history, growth and recent trends in tourism. Definitions of tourism and tourists. Tourism organisations and regulatory bodies, tourist boards, national and international organisations, IATA, UNWTO, CAA, BAA, ABTA, 'Visit Britain' and similar non-UK organisations.	1
The structure of the tourism industry	The role of tour operators and travel agents. The interrelationships and links between the sectors. Travel agents as intermediaries, Tourism distribution channels. Information technology.	2
Governments and political issues	The role of governments and influence on tourism, visas, permits and foreign exchange restrictions. Political unrest. Tourism policy.	5
Tourism ethics and sustainable tourism	Issues in sustainable tourism, sustainable policies and procedures in destinations. Tourism business practices and codes of conduct for ethical tourism.	7
Tourists needs and motivations	The different types and needs of tourists; business and leisure. Reasons for travel and the travel experience for heritage, culture, scenery, weather and facilities. Psychological and sociological influences, facilitators and motivators to encourage travel.	3

Development of tourism destinations	Factors required to become a tourist destination. Development of destinations that meet the needs of tourists. Man-made and natural tourism attractions.	4
Transport and accommodation	Transportation facilities. The range of accommodation available. Grading criteria.	4
Positive and negative economic tourism impacts	**Positive impacts**: direct and indirect income and employment, the multiplier effect, contribution to GDP, currency exchange rates.	6
	Negative impacts: foreign ownership of facilities and hotels, high level of imports of goods for tourism, high demand driven inflation, seasonality, over dependence on tourism industry.	
Positive and negative environmental tourism impacts	**Positive**: conservation of natural beauty areas, archaeological and historic sites, improved infrastructure, environmental awareness.	6
	Negative: pollution, over development leading to destruction of flora and fauna, land use problems, waste disposal, damage to archaeological and historic sites.	
Positive and negative socio-cultural tourism impacts	**Positive**: conservation of cultural heritage, buildings and artefacts, renewal of cultural pride, cross-cultural exchanges.	6
	Negative: overcrowding, over commercialisation, loss of authenticity or customs, social problems, influx of expatriate labour.	

Assessment

This module will be assessed via a 2½ hour examination, set and marked by CTH. The examination will cover the whole of the assessment criteria in this unit and will take the form of 10 x 2 mark questions and 5 x 4 mark questions in section A (40 marks). Section B will comprise of 5 x 20 mark questions of which candidates must select and answer three (60 marks). CTH is a London-based awarding body and the syllabus content will in general reflect this. Any legislation and codes of practice will reflect the international nature of the industry and will not be country specific.

International centres may find it advantageous to add local legislation or practice to their teaching but they should be aware that the CTH examination will not assess this local knowledge.

Further guidance

Recommended contact hours: 45
Credits: 10

Delivery strategies

This module offers an overview of the tourism industry. It is therefore essential that the diversity of the industry is demonstrated through the use of videos, visits to appropriate bodies and the use of guest speakers. Students should be actively involved in their learning and should be encouraged to draw on their work experience in tourism organisations.

Recommended prior learning

There is no required prior learning however students must have completed formal education to 18 years old or equivalent. A keen interest in the tourism industry is essential.

Resources

Learners need access to library and research facilities which should include some or all of the following:

Key text

The Tourism Industry CTH Study Guide (2009), BPP Learning Media, ISBN 9780 7517 7794 9.

Supporting texts

- Cooper, C et al. (2008), *Tourism: Principles and Practice*, Prentice Hall, ISBN 1408200090.

- Holloway, J C (2006), *The Business of Tourism*, Longman, ISBN 0273701614.

- Laws, E (1995), *Tourist Destination Management: Issues, Analysis and Policies*, Routledge, ISBN 0415105919.

- Lickorish, L & Jenkins, C (1997), *An Introduction to Tourism*, Butterworth-Heinneman, ISBN 0750619562.

Magazines, journals and publications

- Tourism Intelligence Quarterly
- Journal of Tourism Management
- Travel Trade Gazette
- Travel Weekly
- Travel section of any quality newspaper

Websites

www.keynote.co.uk	Key note – market information
www.mintel.com	Mintel – provides media, product and consumer information
www.wttc.org	World Travel and Tourism Council
www.statistics.gov.uk	National Statistics Online – official UK statistics
www.tourismconcern.co.uk	Tourism Concern
www.visitbritain.com	Visit Britain

Notes on the recommended texts

This module should be based on the syllabus and the supporting BPP Learning Media CTH Study Guide. The lecturer's lesson plans should be based on the module syllabus and supported by the BPP Learning Media CTH Study Guide for the subject. Lecturers may also use other relevant texts and supplementary material familiar to the lecturer and based on the lecturer's experience. It is not essential to use all the recommended texts and lecturers should use their experience to decide which ones are most appropriate for their students. Where available and appropriate, past module examinations are available to support lecturers.

CTH will always answer any questions from the centre's Head of Department either by e-mail or by phone.

The exam paper

All the CTH examinations for the Diploma in Hotel Management and Diploma in Tourism Management follow the same format.

Exam duration: 2½ hours

Section A

		Marks
Ten	2 mark questions	20
Five	4 mark questions	20
		40

All questions in Section A are compulsory

Section B

Five	20 mark questions (candidates must choose three)	60
		100

Other titles in this series

BPP Learning Media publishes the following titles for the CTH Diploma in Hotel Management:

- Food and Beverage Operations
- Food Hygiene, Health and Safety
- Front Office Operations
- Housekeeping and Accommodation Operations
- Finance for Tourism and Hospitality*
- Introduction to Business Operations*
- Marketing*
- The Tourism Industry*
- The Global Hospitality Industry

*These titles are also papers within the CTH Diploma in Tourism Management qualification.

In July 2010 BPP Learning Media will publish the remaining titles for the Diploma in Tourism Management:

- Travel Geography
- Travel Agency and Tour Guide Operations
- Introduction to Tourism Economics
- Special Interest Tourism
- Destination Analysis

CHAPTER 1

INTRODUCTION TO THE TRAVEL AND TOURISM INDUSTRY

Chapter objectives

In this chapter you will learn to

- Define tourism and tourists
- Investigate the historical growth of tourism
- Identify the different types of tourism
- Investigate the different organisations involved in tourism

Topic list
Definitions of tourism
Different types of tourism
Definitions of tourists
History of tourism development
Tourism organisations

1 Definitions of tourism

1.1 What is tourism?

DEFINITION

"The sum of the phenomena and relationships arising from the travel and stay of non-residents, insofar as they do not lead to permanent residence and are not connected with any earning activity."
Hunziker and Krapf (1941)

"Tourism is the temporary, short-term movement of people to destination outside the places where they normally live and work and their activities during the stay at each destination. It includes movements for all purposes."
Tourism Society of England (1976)

"Particular activities selected by choice and undertaken outside the home environment."
International Association of Scientific Experts in Tourism (1981)

"Tourism comprises the activities of persons travelling to and staying in places outside their usual environment for not more than one consecutive year for leisure, business or other purposes."
UNWTO (1993)

ACTIVITY 1   20 MINUTES

Do you notice any similarities between the definitions? Identify 'key words' from the definitions provided.

As we can see from the definitions, tourism in general has some key factors, but it may not be as simple as it first appears. Subcategories also exist from these main definitions.

2 Different types of tourism

The *United Nations (1994)* identify three forms of tourism:

Domestic tourism: residents travelling only within their country of residence
Inbound tourism: involving non-residents travelling to the given country
Outbound tourism: involving residents travelling to another country

The World Tourism Organisation (UNWTO) also identify different categories of tourism:

Internal tourism: domestic tourism and inbound tourism
National tourism: domestic tourism and outbound tourism
International tourism: inbound tourism and outbound tourism

FOR DISCUSSION

Looking at the different forms of tourism, talk about:

A trip you have made within your own country – Where was it? What did you see?

A journey you have made outside your country – Where did you go? Why did you go?

Visitors you have met in your country – Where were they from? Why were they visiting your country?

BPP
LEARNING MEDIA

3 Definitions of tourists

3.1 What is a tourist?

DEFINITION

The UNWTO identify as a tourist people who *"travel to and stay in places outside their usual environment for not more than one consecutive year for leisure, business and other purposes not related to the exercise of an activity remunerated from within the place visited."* UNWTO (2003)

The World Tourism Organisation (UNWTO), identify two main types of tourists:

International tourist

"A visitor who travels to a country other than that in which he/she has his/her usual residence for at least one night but not more than one year, and whose main purpose of visit is other than the exercise of an activity remunerated within the country visited." UNWTO (1991)

Domestic tourist

"Any person, regardless of nationality, resident in a country and who travels to a place in the same country for not more than one year and whose main purpose of visit is other than following an occupation remunerated from within the place visited." UNWTO (1994)

ACTIVITY 2   10 minutes

Select the key words in all of the definitions – are they the same?

What difference can you identify between a domestic tourist and an international tourist?

FOR DISCUSSION

Have you ever been a domestic tourist, and if yes, why?

Have you ever been an international tourist, why were you an international tourist?

4 History of tourism development

Period	Region	Travel motivation
3,000 BC	Egypt/Babylonia	Business
1,500 BC	Egypt	Religion/leisure and pleasure – Pyramids
6 BC	Egypt	Heritage/culture – 'Museum of Historic Antiquities'
5 BC	Greece	Athens – religion – Panthenon/Acropolis
4 BC	Athens, Sparta, Troy	Guided tours – guidebooks
2 BC	Roman Empire	Roman infantrymen VFR – improved communications
Middle Ages	Europe	'Haligdeg' – 'Holy day' (Holiday) – day of rest – Sunday
16 AD	Europe	'Pilgrimages' – religion: Canterbury, Santiago De Compostela, Rome (via Venice)
C17 – 19th AD	Europe	Culture/education – 'The Grand Tour'

4.1   The Grand Tour

"As such it (the Grand Tour) fulfilled a major social need, namely the necessity of finding young men, who were not obliged to work and for whom work would often be a derogation, something to do between school and the inheritance of family wealth. It allowed the young to sow their wild oats abroad and it kept them out of trouble, including disputes with their family, at home."   *Black (1992)*

- The 'Grand Tour', a term first used by *Richard Lessels* in his book 'Voyage to Italy' (1670), was a 'rite of passage', generally taken by the sons of British, French, German and Russian aristocrats.

- The purpose of the trip, which was normally between six months and three years, was to teach the 'young men' about art, such as the 'Renaissance' artists, antiquities and architecture.

- The most popular cities for these young 'eligible bachelors', were: Florence, Naples, Paris, Rome and Venice.

- The trip increased their knowledge of culture and the arts, and made them more eligible for marriage on their return.

A C T I V I T Y   3   1 0   m i n u t e s

On a map of Europe, locate the 'Grand Tour' city destinations.

Who do you think were these 'young men' who travelled to these destinations?

Some authors liken 'the Grand Tour' to modern-day travel, the 'gap year'.

> **Homework activity**
>
> Go to the website: http://greatgapyears.co.uk
>
> Find out more about 'gap year'
>
> What is it? What types of people go on 'gap years'? Which countries are popular for 'gap years'?

4.2   Health tourism

"Any kind of travel to make one's self or a member of one's family healthier."

Mueller & Kaufmann (2001)

Health tourism has been a very popular form of tourism since the Roman Empire, when Romans used to gather together in communal pools to relax.

> **Homework**
>
> Go to the website: http://www.romanbaths.co.uk and find out more about the history and tourism of Bath.

Later, *Dr William Turner (1562)*, identified the health benefits of '*water as a cure'*, and described the bathing in water as '*taking the cure'*. Many towns and regions in Europe with natural spas began to receive tourists, wanting to 'take the cure', and with this, these areas and towns began to develop their own tourism industry, based on 'health tourism'.

A C T I V I T Y   4   1 5   m i n u t e s

On a map of Europe, locate the following locations that have developed due to 'health tourism' and their natural spa waters.

Town/region	Country
Bath	England
Baden Baden	Germany
Budapest	Hungary
Buxton	England
Frantiskovy Lazne	Czech Republic
Siena	Italy

4.3 Sun, sea and sand (3S's)

The 18th Century saw the decline of inland spa towns, and the growth of seaside tourism, particularly in Europe and the UK. The main reasons for this increase are attributed to:

Enabling factors – factors which make travel possible.

In the 19th Century, better transport and communications enabled faster and cheaper travel. This enabled people to travel more, and led to the development of more and better accommodation to satisfy the increase in demand.

Motivating factors – factors which persuade people to travel.

With the development of industries and the Industrial Revolution many of the residents of Europe's growing cities, in particular in the United Kingdom, had an '**intrinsic need**' to 'get away' from the industrial landscapes of smoke and smog, and escape their physical, labour-intensive jobs.

During the 19th Century, the first passenger railway was established. This led to further developments in the railway networks in mainland Europe, North America and the United Kingdom, with links established between the major urban areas within these regions.

In the United Kingdom, many people began to use the railways (enabling factor) to escape (motivating factor) their industrial cities and towns, to have holidays at the coast, this even included the closing of all the factories in Leicester for two weeks, known as the 'Factory Fortnight'.

ACTIVITY 5   20 minutes

On a map of the United Kingdom, locate the following seaside towns and find the nearest big city from where you think people 'escaped' (motivating factor) to visit the seaside.

Seaside town	City
Brighton	
Blackpool	
Bournemouth	
Great Yarmouth	
Scarborough	
Skegness	
Southend-on-Sea	
Torquay	
Weston-Super-Mare	
Whitley Bay	

4.4 Mass tourism

Mass tourism could be described as tourism involving 'the transportation of large numbers of people to places of leisure interest, to enjoy the benefits of leisure time'. This form of tourism became increasingly popular in the 1960s and 1970s, with an increase in demand for sun, sea and sand (**motivating factor**), and the arrival of cheap package holidays (**enabling factor**).

Case Study – Thomas Cook – 'The Father of the Package Holiday'

1808	Thomas Cook is born on 22 November in the village of Melbourne in Derbyshire.
1841	Organises first excursion, a rail journey from Leicester to a temperance meeting in Loughborough. A special train carries some 500 passengers a distance of 12 miles and back for one shilling.
1845	Thomas Cook conducts his first trip for profit, a railway journey to Liverpool from Leicester, Nottingham and Derby. Fares are 15/- first class and 10/- second class.
1846	Thomas visits Scotland for the first time, with 350 people travelling from Leicester by rail to Glasgow.
1851	Thomas Cook promotes trips to the Great Exhibition in Hyde Park. More than 150,000 people from Yorkshire and the Midlands, travel to London under his arrangements.
1855	First continental tour. He personally conducts two parties from Harwich to Antwerp, then on to Brussels, Cologne, Frankfurt, Heidelberg, Strasbourg and, finally, to Paris for the International Exhibition.
1863	Thomas Cook conducts his first party of 62 people to Switzerland, via Paris.
1865	Thomas Cook opens an office in Fleet Street, London.
1868	Thomas Cook introduces a system of hotel coupons to get fixed prices for accommodation at selected hotels in all major cities.
1869	Thomas Cook escorts his first party to Egypt and Palestine.
1872/73	Thomas Cook organises and leads the first round-the-world tour.
1873	Thomas Cook publishes the first edition of Cook's Continental Time Tables and Tourist's Handbook.
1874	Cook's Circular Note, an early form of the traveller's cheque, is launched in New York.

Source: http://www.thomascook.com/aboutus

Home activity

Visit the website www.thomascook.com/about-us/thomas-cook-history, and find out more about the history and growth of 'Thomas Cook'.

4.5 Other forms of tourism

Culinary tourism	*'The pursuit of unique and memorable eating and drinking experiences'* (International Culinary Tourism Association)
Dark tourism	Travel to sites associated with **death** and **suffering**
Disaster tourism	Travel to areas that have suffered disasters, such as natural disasters
Eco-tourism	Tourism which benefits the community, economy and environment of a local area

Heritage (cultural) tourism	*"Travelling to experience the places and activities that authentically represent the stories and people of the past and present."* (National Trust)
Medical (health) tourism	*"The practice of visiting other countries specifically to benefit from the medical services available there."* (http://encarta.msn.com/dictionary)
Space tourism	*"A commercial venture that carries passengers into space safely and profitably."* (http://www.thespacereview.com)

Homework

Choose two types of tourism as stated in the table above, and find out more about these forms of tourism.

---

5 Tourism organisations

The tourism industry consists of many layers and can be seen as quite a complex industry, which will be further investigated in Chapter 2, but ultimately it can be deemed to consist of three main sectors, and this is the same in most countries throughout the world.

5.1 Private sector

DEFINITION

Private sector tourism companies – '*any company controlled and operated by private individuals (and not by civil servants or government-employees)* (www.businessdictionary.com), are very varied in type and size.

A C T I V I T Y   6   **1 0   m i n u t e s**

In the table below, give an example of a company for each of the types of private tourism organisation.

Type of private tourism organisation	Example
Artificial tourism attraction	
Tour operator	
Transport provider	
Travel agency	

5.2 Public (government) organisations

In most countries throughout the world, there is a government department concerned or dedicated to tourism, and these generally occur at national, regional and local level.

According to *Hall (2000)* the government has eight roles in tourism, including:

- **Co-ordination** – sharing information and co-ordinating with tourism agencies, both public and private, to avoid duplication of resources.

- **Planning** – controlling the development of tourism, determining where and what is appropriate to develop.

- **Legislation and regulation** – includes factors such as: employment, immigration and visa regulations.

- **Stimulation** – stimulating tourism supply by incentives, including: tax relief for tourism developers. Sponsoring research on understanding markets and product innovation, and stimulating demand through marketing and promotion.

- **Marketing and promotion** – trying to increase interest in a destination, including 'destination branding'.

- **Entrepreneurship** – the government own and operate tourism ventures, or own and manage land.

- **Providing social tourism** – providing opportunities for groups of society who are under-privileged or on low incomes.

- **Protector of the public interest** – to act as an 'intermediary' in case of conflict or competing interests.

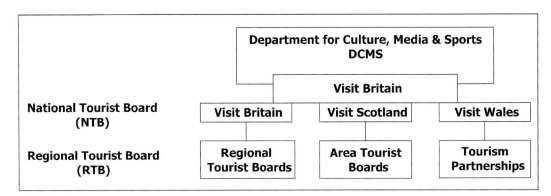

Figure 1.1: The structure of public sector tourism in the UK

Homework

In relation to Figure 1.1 showing the structure of government tourism organisations in the UK, investigate the structure of the public sector of tourism in your own country.

What are the similarities or differences between your own country and the UK?

What are the actions and responsibilities of each level of the government in relation to tourism in your own country?

5.3 Regulatory bodies

Due to the complex nature of the travel and tourism industry and its international scale, there is an obligatory need for standards and regulations to be set. These 'regulatory bodies' enable 'standardisation' at different levels to overcome any misinterpretations that may occur in an industry as complex and grand as the travel and tourism industry.

5.3.1 Public regulatory bodies

International Civil Aviation Organisation (ICAO)

The ICAO aims to ensure "safe, secure and sustainable development of civil aviation through co-operation amongst its member states".

Strategic objectives for the period 2005–2010:

- **Safety** – enhance global civil aviation safety

- **Security** – enhance global civil aviation security

- **Environmental protection** – minimise the adverse effect of global civil aviation on the environment

- **Efficiency** – enhance the efficiency of aviation operations

- **Continuity** – maintain the continuity of aviation operations
- **Rule of Law** – strengthen law governing international civil aviation

Source: www.icao.int

International Air Transport Association (IATA)

IATA mission statement is "to represent, lead and serve the airline industry", and represents "93% of scheduled international air traffic".   *Source:* www.iata.co.uk

- IATA represents consumers by simplifying travel and shipping processes
- IATA allows airlines to operate safely, securely, efficiently and economically under clearly defined rules.
- IATA serves as an intermediary between airlines and passenger as well as cargo agents via neutrally applied agency service standards and centralised financial systems.
- A large network of industry suppliers and service providers gathered by IATA provides solid expertise to airlines in a variety of industry solutions.
- For governments, IATA seeks to ensure they are well informed about the complexities of the aviation industry to ensure better, long-term decisions.

Source: www.iata.co.uk

UFTAA: United Federation of Travel Agents' Associations

Mission statement

"To be an international forum where matters affecting the world travel industry are addressed, representing and defending the interests of incoming and outgoing tour operators, travel and tourism agencies before the governmental bodies, suppliers and other entities of international scope". It also aims at strengthening its members' image and enhance the world travel and tourism industry and sustainable tourism.

Functions of UFTAA

- To unite and consolidate the Federations of Travel Agents' National Associations and globally enhance the interests of their members
- To represent the travel agents' activities before various worldwide bodies, governmental authorities and suppliers
- To work towards the adoption of measures that will ease travel for the consumer and to offer services to its member federations
- To be an investigation and information centre supporting the member Federations' work and to offer information for technological development
- To offer, as a voluntary mechanism, an arbitration service which assists in solving conflicts resulting from commercial relations for which amicable settlement cannot be reached
- To organise a world congress of travel agents and other meetings necessary to the exchange and transmission of knowledge

World Tourism Organisation (UNWTO)

The WTO *"plays a central and decisive role in promoting the development of responsible, sustainable and universally accessible tourism, paying particular attention to the interests of developing countries, and encourages the implementation of the 'Global Code of Ethics for Tourism".*

Source: www.unwto.org

> **Homework**
>
> Visit the World Tourism Organisation (WTO) website (www.unwto.org) and investigate further the work of the WTO, in particular its 'Global Code of Ethics for Tourism'.

5.3.2 Supranational regulating bodies

"Bodies associated with regional trading blocs"   *Hall (2008)*

Supranational bodies cover a number of countries in a particular geographical area, and examples include: Association of South-East Asian Nations (ASEAN), the European Union (EU), and the North American Free Trade Area (NAFTA). For example, in Europe the EU introduced measures to protect travel consumers, which included 'the Package Travel Regulations 1992'.

EU Package Travel Regulations (1992)

- Provide financial protection
- Tour operators provide what is promised

The main provisions are:

- Tour operators are responsible for the safety of their customers
- Tour operators must give accurate brochure descriptions
- Last-minute surcharges cannot be imposed
- A guaranteed refund if a tour operator becomes bankrupt

> **Homework**
>
> Find out further information about the work of other supranational bodies in relation to tourism regulation and legislation.
>
> Is there anything similar to the 'package travel regulations'? Or are there different regulations that exist in these regional trading blocs?

5.3.3 National regulatory bodies

On a national level there are numerous organisations that help to regulate and monitor the travel and tourism industry, this generally involves governments, and various national bodies to ensure standards are maintained on a national level. The following table shows some of the national regulatory bodies in the United Kingdom (UK).

Name	Description
Association of British Travel Agents (ABTA) (www.abta.com)	*"To maintain high standards of trading practice for the benefit of members, the travel industry, the consumers that they serve, and create as favourable a business climate as possible for its members".*
Air Transport Operators Licence (ATOL) (www.caa.co.uk)	All tour operators and travel firms selling air holiday packages and flight in the UK are required by law to hold a licence called an Air Travel Organiser's Licence.
Civil Aviation Authority (CAA) (www.caa.co.uk)	Independent aviation regulator, whose main concerns are: • Air safety • Airspace regulation • Consumer protection • Economic regulation • Environmental research and consultancy

ACTIVITY 7   2 0 minutes

Investigate national regulatory bodies within your own country, and compare and contrast these with one of the regulatory bodies in the table.

SUMMARY

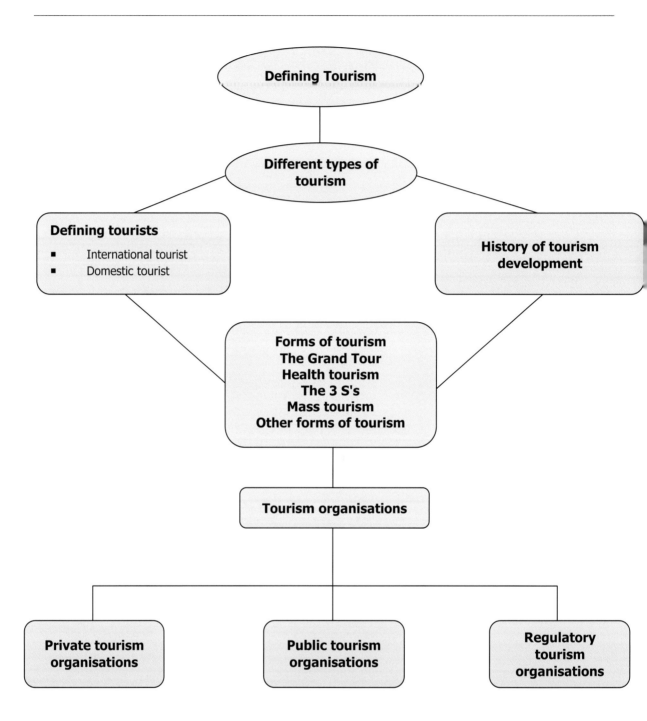

SELF-TEST QUESTIONS

1   Give a definition of tourism.

2   Identify the differences between an international tourist and a domestic tourist.

3   What is 'the Grand Tour', and give examples of destinations of this form of tourism.

4   What do you understand by the terms: enabling factors and motivating factors?

5   Define in your own words 'mass tourism'.

6   What do you understand by the term 'package tour'?

7   Identify three 'other' forms of tourism, and briefly explain each one.

8   Provide some examples of private tourism organisations, with industry examples.

9   Identify some of the functions of 'public' sector tourism organisations.

10   What do you understand by the following acronyms/abbreviations:

- NTB
- RTB

11   Identify the following international regulatory body acronyms and briefly explain the role of each one:

- ICAO
- IATA
- UFTAA
- WTO

12   What do you understand by the term 'supranational', and provide appropriate examples.

13   What do the following acronyms stand for?

- ABTA
- ATOL
- CAA

14   Briefly describe the role of each of the organisations as mentioned above.

SELF-TEST ANSWERS

1 The answer should try to include the highlighted words from the definition below.

"Tourism comprises the activities of persons travelling to and staying in places outside their usual environment for not more than one consecutive year for leisure, business or other purposes"

UNWTO (1993)

2 You should identify that an international tourist visits a country outside the borders of the country in which they live, and a domestic tourist travels to a destination within the country where they live.

3 The 'Grand Tour' was an educational trip for the sons of British, French, German and Russian aristocrats to teach them about art, such as the 'Renaissance' artists, antiquities and architecture, and included journeys to cities such as: Florence, Naples, Paris, Rome and Venice.

4 Enabling factors 'Pull Factors' are factors which make travel possible, and attract the traveller to a particular destination', this can include transport and access. Motivating Factors 'Push Factors' are the factors which persuade people to travel to a particular destination, such as the destination being cheap due to exchange rates or having a very favourable climate.

5 Your answer should include: tourism to destinations where lots of tourists visit, and the destination is fully developed to meet the needs of the high numbers of tourists that visit.

6 A 'package tour' is a holiday that consists of two or more elements, and generally includes transport to and from the destination and accommodation within the destination, sold at one price to the customer.

7 Examples of other types of tourism can include: culinary tourism, dark tourism, disaster tourism, eco-tourism, heritage (cultural) tourism, medical (health) tourism and space tourism.

8 Some examples of 'private tourism organisations' includes: artificial tourist attraction, such as a theme park, tour operators such as TUI, transport provider, such as an airline eg British Airways and travel agencies, such as Thomas Cook.

9 Some of the functions of 'public' or government organisations include: marketing and promoting a destination, laws and regulations and planning for tourism.

10 What do you understand by the following acronyms/abbreviations:

(a)   NTB stands for National Tourist Board, responsible for tourism in a country at a national level.
(b)   RTB means Regional Tourist Board, and they are responsible for tourism at a regional level.

11 The ICAO stands for the International Civil Aviation Organisation, and their aim is for the safe, secure and sustainable development of civil aviation. IATA, International Air Transport Association and their mission is "to represent, lead and serve the airline industry". UFTAA: the United Federation of Travel Agents' Associations unite and consolidate the Federations of Travel Agents' National Associations and globally enhance the interests of their members. The WTO World Tourism Organisation plays a central and decisive role in promoting the development of responsible, sustainable and universally accessible tourism.

12 Supranational are generally regarded as "bodies associated with regional trading blocs" *Hall (2008)*, and examples include: Association of South-East Asian Nations (ASEAN), the European Union (EU), and the North American Free Trade Area (NAFTA).

13 ABTA stands for Association of British Travel Agents, ATOL means Air Transport Operators Licence, and the CAA refers to the Civil Aviation Authority.

14 ABTA maintains standards in the travel agency industry. ATOL is a licence that must be held by any organisation that wishes to sell holiday packages, to determine that the organisation is a reputable company. The CAA ensure that standards of safety and regulations are maintained in the aviation industry.

ANSWERS TO ACTIVITIES

1 Similarities of the key words between the definitions of tourism include:

- Travel and stay of non-residents.

- The temporary, short-term movement of people to destinations outside the places where they normally live and work.

- Persons travelling to and staying in places outside their usual environment.

2 Similarities between the definitions of tourists include:

- Travels to and stay in places outside their usual environment for not more than one consecutive year.

- A visitor who travels to a country other than that in which he/she has his/her usual residence for at least one night but not more than one year.

- Travels to a place in the same country for not more than one year.

The difference between a domestic and an international tourist is that a domestic tourist travels to a destination within the country where they are resident, whereas an international tourist to a destination outside their country of residence.

3 The young men were wealthy aristocrats, from Britain, France, Germany and Russia.

The main 'Grand Tour' destinations are shown below.

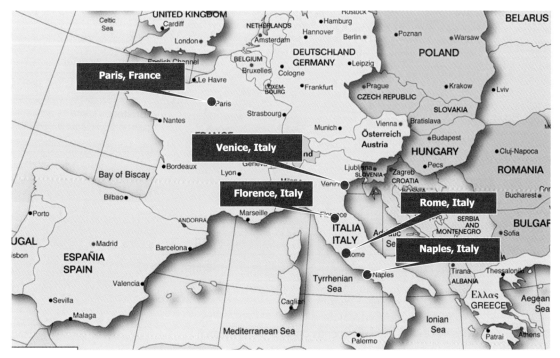

4

5

Seaside town	City
Brighton	London
Blackpool	Manchester
Bournemouth	Southampton
Great Yarmouth	Derby, Nottingham, Norwich
Scarborough	Leeds, Sheffield
Skegness	Derby, Nottingham, Leicester
Southend-on-Sea	London
Torquay	Portsmouth, Bristol
Weston-Super-Mare	Bristol
Whitley Bay	Newcastle

6

Type of Private Tourism Organisation	Example
Artificial Tourist Attraction	Disneyland
Tour Operator	TUI
Transport Provider	British Airways
Travel Agency	Thomas Cook

7 The answer to this activity depends on your own research.

CHAPTER 2

STRUCTURE OF THE TOURISM INDUSTRY

Chapter objectives

In this chapter you will learn to

- Investigate the structure of the tourism industry
- Determine the tourism supply chain
- Identify tourism industry integration
- Understand the influence of information technology (IT) in the tourism industry

Topic list

The structure of the tourism industry
Private sector tourism organisations
Tourism industry integration
Indirect tourism supply chain
Tourism and information technology

1 The structure of the tourism industry

Tourism is one of the world's largest industries, accounting to "*over 10% of gross domestic product*" (GDP) *Cooper et al. (2005)*, and providing employment for a very large number of people: "*tourism employs 8% of the global workforce*" (www.tourismconcern.org.uk). Due to the nature and global scale of the industry, **it is a very complex and multi-faceted industry**.

1.1 The tourism supply chain

"All the goods and services that go into the delivery of tourism products to consumers. It includes all suppliers of goods and services whether or not they are directly contracted...Tourism supply chains involve many components" .

Tapper and Font (2004)

1.1.1 Direct tourism supply chain

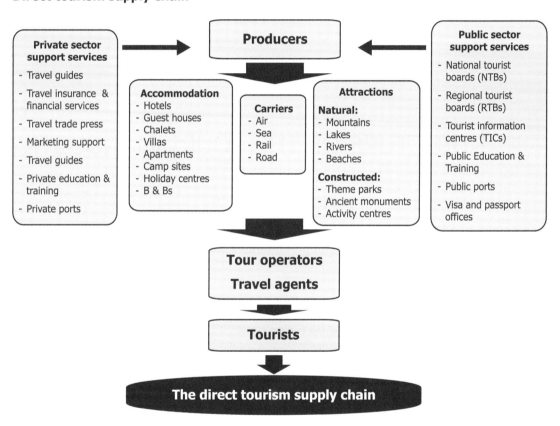

Figure 2.1: The direct tourism supply chain, adapted from *Holloway (2006)*

2 Private sector tourism organisations

Most organisations within the tourism sector are privately owned and "*driven by profit motives*" *(Page & Connell, 2006)*. These include organisations such as: travel insurance and financial services, travel trade press (newspapers/magazines), marketing support, travel guide publishers, private colleges and private ports. But the most popular forms of 'private tourism organisations' are: tour operators and travel agents.

2.1 Tour operator

DEFINITION

Tour operator – *'purchase separate elements of transport, accommodation and other services, and combine them into a package, which they then sell directly or indirectly to consumers.'*

Holloway (2002)

Normally packages have at least two elements, generally consisting of transport and accommodation, including an overnight stay, which they then sell as an 'all inclusive tour' to consumers. Tour operators can be small, independent tour operators 'specialised tour operators', or large 'transnational' tour operators, who operate globally.

Transport

Accommodation

Overseas representative

Airport transfers

PACKAGE HOLIDAY

Figure 2.2: The elements of an 'all inclusive' package holiday

A C T I V I T Y   1   **1 0   m i n u t e s**

Think of an example of a 'specialised tour operator' and a 'transnational' tour operator. Investigate the types of holidays and destinations of these types of tour operators.

What differences do you notice between these types of tour operators?

2.2 Travel agencies

DEFINITION

"A travel agent or travel agency is a shop or office where you can go to arrange a holiday or journey."
(Collins English Dictionary)

"A business that attends to the details of transportation, itinerary, and accommodation for travellers."
(thefreedictionary.com)

Travel agencies are the 'retail' sector of the 'tourism supply chain,' therefore they sell holidays to consumers, generally from a shop. Travel agencies can fall into three categories:

Travel agency	
Multiple	A travel agency that can be found in many different areas of a country. A national 'chain' of branches that offer a lot of products and services in all their shops.
Miniple	A 'Miniple' has many branches in a particular region. These 'travel agencies' may have started with one shop and one owner, but over time have grown, due to their knowledge of their local market. They may offer less services than 'multiple' travel agencies.
Independent	Generally, these are travel agencies with only one shop. They offer a limited number of services, which may be 'specialised'. Possibly a family-owned or sole-trader business.

FOR DISCUSSION

Travel agencies sell holidays and travel tickets, but they can also offer other services. Discuss the other 'add-on' services that a travel agency can offer to its customers.

3 Tourism industry integration

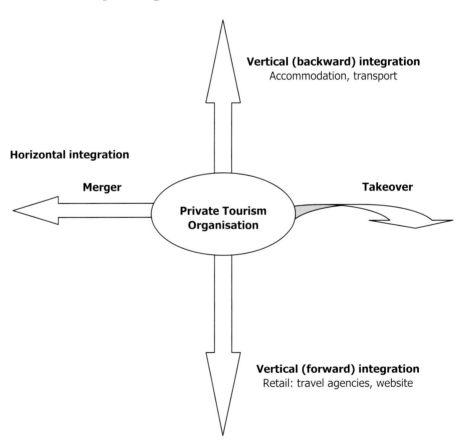

Figure 2.3: Integration strategies for a private tourism organisation

3.1 Vertical integration

> **Vertical integration** – *"when one organisation at one level in the chain of distribution unites with one at another level"*
>
> *Holloway (2006)*

Vertical backward integration

This is when a tour operator buys and subsequently owns the 'elements' needed to make a package holiday. An example could be when a tour operator buys an airline or possibly a group of hotels, but more often tour operators create their own airlines.

FOR DISCUSSION

Think of a tour operator that owns its own airline.

Why do you think some tour operators own their own airlines?

Vertical forward integration

Forward or downward integration is more common than backward (upward) integration, and involves the tour operator buying or creating its own travel agencies. In more recent years, forward integration includes a company having its own website, where its can sell its products and services direct to consumers, without the need for a retail shop (travel agency).

FOR DISCUSSION

What are the advantages of tour operators owning their own travel agencies?

Why do tour operators have their own websites?

3.2 Horizontal integration (mergers and acquisition (M & A))

> **Horizontal integration** – *"where two companies offering competing products merge (fuse) or one takes over another"*
>
> *Dale (2005)*

Merger

A merger is when two or more companies, offering similar products or at the same stage of production, come together to become one company. For example, two airlines who operate similar routes may decide to become one airline, or two hotels in the same seaside resort may decide to become one larger hotel chain.

FOR DISCUSSION

What are the opportunities and challenges of mergers for organisations?

How would the employees in the organisations be affected by a merger?

Takeover (acquisitions)

A 'takeover' is when one company buys and takes control of another organisation. This can be a company at the same stage of production, for example an airline buying another airline and becoming one company. It can also happen at a different stage of production, for example a tour operator acquiring an airline, and the airline being owned by the tour operator.

FOR DISCUSSION

Discuss the impacts a takeover has on the company being taken over (acquired).

3.3   Other private sector tourism support services

Private tourism support services	
Travel guides	Published books to provide visitors with information about a particular destination, including: transport, things to do, things to see, expressions etc. Examples include: Lonely Planet, Rough Guides.
Travel insurance and financial services	Many financial institutions, such as banks, provide services for tourists, this can include: 'Bureau de change', where tourists can exchange money, and travel insurance to cover tourists in case of an accident while on holiday, examples include: Columbus direct, the AA and many banks.
Travel trade press	There are a number of magazines, newspapers published for travel and tourism professionals, providing up-to-date articles and reviews on industry news: *Travel Trade Gazette* and *The Caterer* are two examples.
Marketing support	Some private companies provide 'marketing support' for both private and public tourism organisations. These 'consulting' companies can give advice on marketing strategies and help collect data for tourism and travel organisations, examples include: 'The Tourism Company' and 'The Tourism Network'.
Private education and training	Many private education institutions provide qualifications and training for 'would-be' tourism professionals, this can include schools which offer courses such as: 'Virgin Atlantic' ticketing and fares.
Private ports	Some 'ports' (access point), are owned by private companies and individuals. Shipping companies must pay these private organisations to use their 'port facilities' and to load and unload freight.

3.4   Accommodation

Continuing with the 'private sector' of tourism producers is the accommodation factor, and in respect of the numerous definitions of accommodation, this generally means a place where tourists are provided with somewhere to sleep. Accommodation can take many forms, depending on location and size of the destination, but the following table provides some examples of different types of accommodation.

Accommodation types	
Catered	**Self-catering**
Hotels	**Apartments, villas, gites, cottages**
Formal accommodation offering full services.	Privately-owned by individuals or companies, where the guests provide their own food and do their own cooking
These can include: 'Country House Hotels' with big gardens set in the countryside or a 'Metro Hotel' which can be found in a city centre.	
Guest houses	**Campus accommodation**
Accommodation for more than six paying guests, with the owner and staff providing more services, for example, dinner.	University halls of residences, where tourists can rent rooms, during non-term time.
Bed and Breakfast (B&B)	**Youth hostel**
Accommodation provided in a private house by the owner for up to six paying guests.	Generally basic accommodation, where guests stay in dormitories or rooms with other people and kitchen facilities are provided.
Farmhouses	**Camp sites**
B&B or guest house accommodation provided on a working farm.	Privately-owned land, where tourists pay a nightly-fee to pitch their tent or caravan, with washing and electricity sometimes provided.

Other accommodation

Time-share – tourists pay for access to an apartment for a set date over a number of years.

Cruise liners and ferries – on long distance journeys, passengers are provided with a cabin.

Trains and aircraft – Long-distance journeys can be provided with sleeping accommodation, such as couchettes (sleeping carriages) or seats that recline into beds.

FOR DISCUSSION

Think of a time when you have stayed in any of the above types of accommodation. Which destination were you in? Did you have food provided or did you have to cook your own food? Was it large accommodation or did you rent it with your family?

3.5 Carriers

These are the transport companies that 'carry' us, from our home environment to the destination. Generally, these consist of four transport types:

AIr	This includes all the air travel that enables very quick transportation within our own country (domestic) or to a different country (abroad).
Sea	Transportation across water that can include ferries, cruise ships or yachts.
Rail	Transportation across land that can take us to our destination or can be the holiday itself. Some trains provide catering and sleeping accommodation for passengers.
Road	Road transport can include many different types, including buses and coaches, for airport transfers, coach holidays or just getting to a destination, cars, such as private cars or car rental, motorbikes and bicycles, which can be hired at a destination.

FOR DISCUSSION

Can you name any 'private' companies that provide the types of transportation as detailed above.

Have you ever taken any of these types of transport? Where were you going? Why did you take this form of transport?

3.6 Attractions

DEFINITION

Attraction – *"a named site with a specific human or natural feature which is the focus of visitor and management attention."*

As we can see from the definition, attractions generally fall into two main categories: constructed (man-made) or natural, and can be controlled, managed and owned by a 'private' company or by a 'public' organisation, the government.

ACTIVITY 2   20 minutes

In the table, give some examples of constructed (man-made) and natural attractions.

Natural	Constructed (man-made)

Which attractions do you think are owned and managed by the government and which ones do you think are managed by private companies?

4 Indirect tourism supply chain involvement

Tourism also impacts upon other sectors, and the tourism industry would not be able to develop and function without these other sectors.

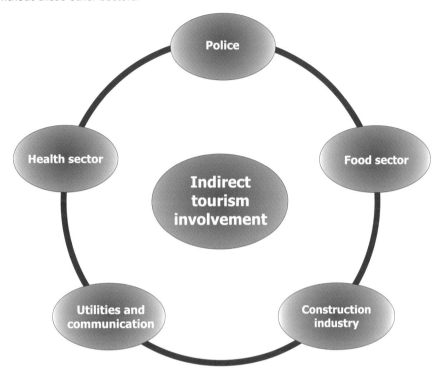

Figure 2.4: Indirect tourism involvement adapted from *Page and Connell (2006)*

Health sector

This includes hospitals and medical centres, which are needed in tourist areas to deal with accidents that may occur. This may include tourists having medical needs for things such as 'food poisoning', bites, sunburn or accidents that may occur due to water-sports or transport.

Police

A police force is very important in tourist areas, as tourism due to its nature, attracts a lot of people to one destination. The police provide security, deal with problems such as: robbery and theft, and control large groups of people in one area.

Food sector

The food sector or catering industry is one of the most important elements in the travel and tourism industry. This includes restaurants and take-away outlets, but it can also include catering providers to hotels and airlines.

Construction industry

Without builders and engineers, destinations would be unable to develop. The construction industry provides a destination with the 'infrastructure', sewerage, drainage, hotels, roads and airports, and the 'superstructure', shops, restaurants and attractions, to enable tourists to be accommodated and entertained during their stay.

Utilities and communication

This includes 'public utilities' such as water, drainage, sewerage, electricity, which are provided for locals and for the increased population of tourists in a region. Locals and ever increasingly tourists need more and newer forms of communication, therefore, telephone lines and cables need to be provided to enable people to make telephone calls or send e-mails, and even for tourism companies to communicate to their headquarters which may be in a different country.

All of these factors add to the tourism 'multiplier effect', and without this 'indirect tourism involvement' many functions of the tourism industry would be impossible to be carried out.

A C T I V I T Y   3   2 0   m i n u t e s

Think of a time when you were on holiday.

Did you ever use one of the 'indirect tourism support services; as mentioned above?

Why did you have to use this service?

5   Tourism and information technology (IT)

Information technology has become increasingly important in the travel and tourism industry, both for tourism organisations and tourists.

5.1   Tourists and IT

More and more tourists are using the internet to book holidays. The internet allows tourists to sit at home and search for 'package holidays' on tour operators' websites, or they can book their own itineraries for their own needs 'tailor made'. Many tourists find their own flights from 'web-based' airlines, and print off their own tickets 'e-tickets'. Tourists can also search the internet for accommodation, using hotel companies' websites or with accommodation search engines, which will search for accommodation to meet the individual needs and requirements of the tourists.

5.2   Tourism organisations and IT

Many tourism and hospitality companies use IT for their organisational purposes. This includes: having their own websites, where tourists can book directly without the need for an agent 'dis-intermediation'. Many tourism and hospitality organisations also use IT for marketing, customer reservations (CRS), including 'Galileo', Amadeus, and at some airports customers can check-in without the need of a check-in agent 'self-check-in'.

F O R   D I S C U S S I O N

Have you ever used the internet to book a holiday or a flight?

What do you think are the advantages of using the internet for purchasing 'tourism-related' products?

S U M M A R Y

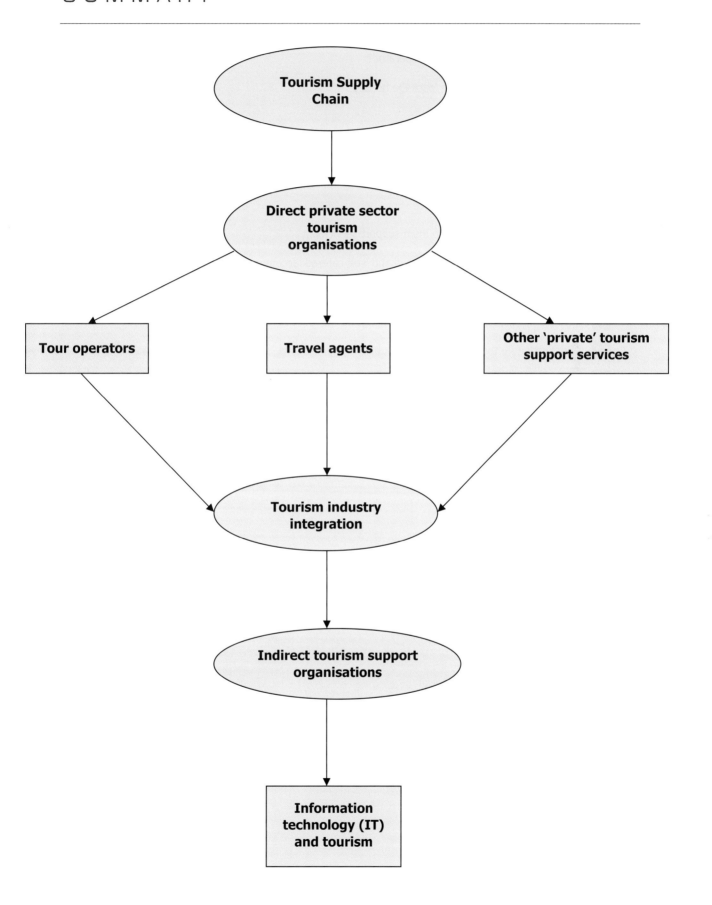

SELF-TEST QUESTIONS

1   What is the function of a 'tour operator'?

2   With examples, describe a 'package holiday'.

3   What is a travel agent?

4   Name the three different types of 'travel agencies'.

5   What is 'vertical integration'?

6   What is 'horizontal integration'?

7   Name three other private tourism support services.

8   Provide some examples of 'catered' and 'self-catered' accommodation.

9   Name the four transportation carriers.

10   With examples, name the two main categories of tourist attractions.

11   Briefly identify the 'indirect tourism support' organisations.

12   Provide examples of tourism products consumers can purchase on the internet.

BPP LEARNING MEDIA

SELF-TEST ANSWERS

1 The function of a tour operator is to *'purchase separate elements of transport, accommodation and other services, and combine them into a package, which they then sell directly or indirectly to consumers.'*

Holloway (2002)

2 A 'package holiday' generally consists of four elements: transport, accommodation, the services of an overseas representative and transfers to and from the airport, which are all included for sale at one single price.

3 A travel agent is a person that works in a travel agency and sells transportation itinerary and accommodation for travellers.

4 The three types of travel agencies are: multiple, miniple and independent.

5 Vertical integration is when one organisation at one level in the chain of distribution unites with one at another level. This can include a tour operator that owns its own airline (backward) or travel agency (forward).

6 Horizontal integration is where two companies offering competing products merge (fuse) or one takes over another, examples can include airlines merging to become one larger airline or a tour operator buying a smaller tour operator.

7 Three examples of private tourism support services can include: travel trade press, travel marketing services and education and training providers.

8 Catered accommodation can include: bed and breakfasts (B&B), guest houses and hotels. Examples of 'self-catered' accommodation include: apartments, hostels and campsites.

9 The four transportation carriers are: air, rail, road and sea.

10 The two main categories of tourist attractions are: natural, for example mountains, and man-made such as a water-park.

11 Indirect tourism support services include: the health sector, the police, food sector, the construction industry and communications and utilities.

12 Examples of tourism products that can be purchased on the internet include: airline tickets (e-tickets), accommodation, transfers and ancillary services such as insurance and car hire.

ANSWERS TO ACTIVITIES

1 Answer depends on your own research.

2 Examples of constructed (man-made) and natural attractions, can include:

Natural	Constructed (Man-made)
Beaches	Theme parks
Rivers	Water parks
Mountains	Museums
Lakes	Art galleries
Caves	Theatres

3 The answer to this activity will depend on your personal experience.

CHAPTER 3

TOURIST NEEDS AND MOTIVATIONS

Chapter objectives

In this chapter you will learn to

- Investigate travel motivations
- Identify different types of tourists
- Understand different tourist needs
- Determine the constraints on tourist motivations

1   Tourist motivations and needs

Why do people go on holiday? What are their needs when they are deciding where to go on holiday? These are questions that tourism academics and tourism organisations, both public and private, have been discussing for many years, and will probably continue discussing as long as people travel.

A C T I V I T Y   1   **1 5   m i n u t e s**

Think of the different reasons why people travel (travel motivations), and provide examples of destinations for each of the tourist motivations.

Think of the last time you travelled. Why did you travel? Why did you go to that destination?

The reason why a person travels is termed the **'push factor'** (why did you travel?), and the motive for going to a particular destination is deemed the **'pull factor'** (why did you go to that destination?).

Dann (1977)

1.1   Travel motivations

DEFINITION

Motivation – "*a state of need, a condition that exerts a push on the individual towards certain types of action that are seen as likely to bring satisfaction.*"

Mouthino (1987)

As we can see from the definition, a motivation is something that we may need, and to satisfy this need some form of action is needed. The following provides some examples of why people travel.

Travel motivation	
Business	Many people have to travel for their work. This can include meetings and conferences, to meet clients and to 'network'. This form of tourism can be termed: MICE tourism; Meetings, Incentives, Conferences and Exhibitions.
Culture	People may want to travel to learn about: architecture, food and drink, lifestyle and religion. They want to visit a place to learn more about the culture and history of a destination (wanderlust).
Desire for adventure	Some people travel to a different place to experience something new or different to what they can experience in their home environment. This can involve 'active activities' such as a safari or extreme sports.
Education	Many tourists travel to other countries for educational purposes, this could be to learn a new language or to study at a famous university or in a famous city.
Escape	Often tourists want to escape their routine 'the rat race' of work or even their home environment, just to have a change of scenery. 'A change is as good as a rest.'
Love and romance	This generally involves travel to romantic or exotic places, and can possibly include 'honeymoons' or even weddings on the beach in exotic environments.
Physical reasons	Many people may want to get away for some rest and relaxation (R & R), having worked hard all year. The holiday may involve very 'passive activities', such as reading and laying on a beach (sunlust).
Social reasons	Some tourists like to go on holiday to meet other people, and make new friends. This could involve holidays to destinations with lots of nightlife and social activities or visiting friends and relatives (VFR).

FOR DISCUSSION

Think of a travel destination for each of the travel motivations as identified in the table above, and discuss why you think this is an appropriate destination for the tourist motivation type.

ACTIVITY 2   30 minutes

As tabled below, for each of the people, match a holiday suitable to their needs.

People	Holiday
1 James and Alison want to celebrate their first wedding anniversary. James wants to surprise Alison with a weekend away.	a A few days in Brighton, staying at a 5-star sea-front hotel with spa facilities.
2 Jonathan, a tourism lecturer, wants to take his tourism class on a 'field trip'.	b A weekend 'city-break' in Barcelona.
3 Paul is having problems with his teeth, but dentists are very expensive in the UK.	c Five days on the 'Costa Brava' in Spain, to include visits to some hotels and talks from a holiday representative.
4 A group of six friends, who regularly go out at weekends, want to go away together for two weeks on a 'lad's holiday'.	d Flight only to Delhi.
5 Joanne is exhausted; she has spent the last six months looking after her baby. Her mother can look after her baby so she can 'go away' for a few days with her husband.	e A weekend in Paris including a boat trip on the River Seine.
6 Vikas and Raj have been studying in London, and have not seen their parents for two years.	f A two week half-board package holiday to Ibiza, with lots of bars and clubs.
7 Robert is having a 'gap year' after working in the city for five years. He wants to 'escape' the 'rat race' routine of work.	g A package to Poland including transport and dental work.
8 John and Rachel, both architects, have been working hard and want to 'get away' and visit some art galleries and museums.	h A round-the-world ticket and a backpack.

Match the following 'motivating factors' to the people listed above.

- Education
- Relaxation
- Romance
- Duty (VFR)

- Social
- Wanderlust
- Culture
- Health

In respect of the nature and globalised scale of the tourism industry, we can determine that people travel for numerous reasons. With these varying tourist motivations, we can identify different groups of tourists, or 'tourist typologies'.

To help interpret the numerous reasons for people travelling, various academics identified the different tourist types or tourist typologies.

2 Tourist typologies

Gray (1970) identified two 'tourist typologies':

- "**Sunlust**" travel undertaken for 'rest and relaxation'.
- "**Wanderlust**", travel undertaken for the 'desire to learn'.

Ploy (1973) further expanded on this by categorising tourists into five types:

Allocentric   **Near-allocentric**   **Mid-centric**   **Near-psychocentric**   **Psychocentric**

Allocentric: These types of tourists can be described as 'explorers', they are people who travel independently, and want to see and do new things. Generally allocentrics have above-average incomes, and they travel to learn 'wanderlust'.

Near-allocentric: These are 'explorers' of a type, but generally go to a destination, once it has been discovered by the allocentrics. Again they are people who desire a 'new experience', and to learn something new.

Mid-centric: The majority of tourists. Generally people who like some adventure, but want some luxuries and organisation; such as excursions to cultural, historical sites. Authenticity is important to a certain extent.

Near-psychocentric: These tourist types are not interested in local culture and customs and want an experience similar to their home environment, including familiar food, music and culture.

Psychocentric: These are tourists who only like familiar environments or cultures therefore they may select a destination which is familiar and possibly not too far from home. They are not interested in the local culture and authenticity is not welcomed.

Familiarity

- **Recreational** – go on holiday to relax, playful and accept inauthentic entertainment.
- **Diversionary** – look for 'escape', diversion from work and normal lives, not interested in authenticity.
- **Experiential** – look for meaning in others lives, and like authenticity.
- **Experimental** – 'experience' different lifestyles and authenticity in the destination visited.
- **Existential** – to live as a 'native' in the visited destination, they demand authenticity.

Novelty

Cohen (2004)

FOR DISCUSSION

Using the different tourist types, identify a destination and choose which type of tourist would go to this destination, and explain why.

Country/destination

Tourist type

What type of tourist are you? Complete *Plog's* 'Your travel personality quiz'.

	Strongly disagree						Strongly agree
	1	2	3	4	5	6	7
I am more intellectually curious than most people I know	☐	☐	☐	☐	☐	☐	☐
I prefer to go to undiscovered places before big hotels and restaurants are built	☐	☐	☐	☐	☐	☐	☐
I prefer to travel independently rather than with a group of people	☐	☐	☐	☐	☐	☐	☐
I make decisions quickly and easily rather than deliberating over them	☐	☐	☐	☐	☐	☐	☐
I find that I often get bored at parties that most people seem to enjoy	☐	☐	☐	☐	☐	☐	☐
I often buy new products before they become popular or come down in price	☐	☐	☐	☐	☐	☐	☐
I have much more energy than most persons my age	☐	☐	☐	☐	☐	☐	☐
I am actively involved in a regular, rigorous fitness programme	☐	☐	☐	☐	☐	☐	☐
My personal interests and pastimes are quite different and novel from what others do	☐	☐	☐	☐	☐	☐	☐
I have friends over to my house frequently	☐	☐	☐	☐	☐	☐	☐
Chance has little to do with success in my life	☐	☐	☐	☐	☐	☐	☐
I will hurry to places even when I have plenty of time	☐	☐	☐	☐	☐	☐	☐
I prefer being around people most of the time	☐	☐	☐	☐	☐	☐	☐
I go out socially with friends quite often	☐	☐	☐	☐	☐	☐	☐
I would rather go for a walk than read a book	☐	☐	⦿	☐	☐	☐	☐

Source: http://host2.dynamicsurveys.com/cgi-bin/survey

Figure 3.1: Plog's travel personality quiz

2.1 Tourist needs

As we have identified there are numerous theories on different tourist types, but there are a lot of reasons why there are different types of tourists. We all have varying needs as people depending on our circumstances, and this is also the same for tourists.

FOR DISCUSSION

Identify the different needs people have when they are considering a holiday or on holiday.

3 Maslow's Hierarchy of Needs (1954)

Self-actualisation
Experience purpose, meaning and realising all inner potentials

Self-esteem
The need to be a unique individual with self-respect and to enjoy general esteem from others

Love and belonging
The need for belonging, to receive and give love, appreciation, friendship

Safety needs
The basic need for social security in a family and a society that protects against hunger and violence

Physiological needs
The need for food, water, shelter and clothing

Figure 3.2: Hierarchy of needs

Maslow's Hierarchy of Needs, a method normally used in motivational theories, has often been applied to tourism psychologies. This theory highlights that different types of tourists have different needs. In relation to Maslow's theory, the needs at the bottom (physiological needs) have to be satisfied, once the tourist has these needs, then they can move up to higher level needs.

- *Physiological/basic needs:* basic needs for existence: food, shelter, warmth, rest.
- *Safety/security needs:* feeling secure, not threatened.
- *Belonging/love/social needs:* friendships, building relationships.
- *Esteem needs:* self-confidence, reputation, prestige.
- *Self-actualisation needs:* 'self-fulfilment' achieving something, and helping others.

ACTIVITY 3   30 minutes

Looking at Maslow's Hierarchy of Needs, give examples in a tourism context for each of the needs, for example a basic need could include a 'tent', to represent shelter.

What do you think 'self-actualisation' needs could be?

For each of the levels of the needs, identify the tourist type and explain your choice.

3.1 Constraints on tourist motivations

As we have determined there are different tourist types and motivations for travel, and certain needs have to be satisfied for these tourist typologies and motivations, but these are very general and sometimes they do not consider certain factors, other factors can influence tourist motivation albeit on a more personal level.

Page & Connell (2006), identify two categories:

- Personal and family influences.
- Social and situational influences.

4 Personal and family influences

Age	Many tour operators and travel organisations, segment their products based on age. Younger adults may be attracted to more 'active holidays', or entertainment, eg Club 18-30, whereas older tourists may want holidays that involve more 'passive' pursuits or more safe and secure activities.
Family life cycle	The stage at which a family is at or 'The Family Life Cycle' can influence the motivation. A family with young children will want to go to a destination with lots of activities for children or 'Kids Clubs'. Teenagers may want 'clubs/bars', not attractions that perhaps would be appreciated by retirees. Therefore, age can be a major determinant on where people go on holiday.
Gender	Women: Voluntary work, getting away from caring (spa breaks) *(Kinnaird & Hall, 1994)*. Lone travel – brave, not normal, vulnerable *(Kinnaird & Hall, 1994)*. More passive activities *(Foo et al, 2004)*. Men: More lone travel – more acceptable – adventurous, more active pursuits – 'adventure holidays' *(Foo et al, 2004)*.
Disability	Some barriers exist for less-abled persons: - Internal: ineffective social skills, health, physical, psychological - Economic: need travel companions, special facilities - Environmental: architectural, accessibility, ecological – paths, hills, transport, rules and regulations, safety. - Interactive: communication, attitudes of industry workers, information availability/accuracy.

Adapted from *Murray & Sproats (1990)*

4.1 The family life cycle

Stage	Characteristics	Tourism behaviour
Early childhood	Entirely dependent on parent or guardian. Classic Sun, Sea and Sand (3 Ss) holiday.	Seaside or inland resort, with entertainment for children.
Early teenager	More influence on decision-making, but still dependent on parents.	Resort-based holidays with nightlife. Group-based holidays.
Young person	Young, single, not living at home.	Sunlust – Wanderlust. Adventure, backpacking and experiences.
Partnership stage	Couples living together, 'young professionals'. Time constraints on travel.	All types of holidays, many short breaks 'city breaks', to fit-in with careers.
Family stage – early	Families, single parents, separated with young children.	Main holidays (mass tourism) and Visiting Friends and Relatives (VFR).
Family stage – late	With children at secondary school, only take holidays outside term-time.	Mix of holidays, children wanting a bit of independence – activities, clubs…
Empty nest	Children leave home, parents more freedom and disposable income.	More expensive holidays: long-haul, cruises, and second breaks.
Retired	One person or partners retired, income fixed, lots of free-time.	More passive, better quality holidays.

Figure 3.3: The family life cycle (North American/European Model) – Lumsdon (1997)

A C T I V I T Y   4   **2 0   m i n u t e s**

For each of the different stages above, think of an appropriate destination, giving consideration to why it is suitable.

5 Social and situational issues

Nationality and national identity	This can include:
	Language barriers – which may discourage some people to travel abroad.
	Legal requirements – visa acquisition difficulties may prevent, deter travel for some nationalities.
Tourism and work	**Time** – the more people work, the less time they have to travel and vice-versa.
	Nature of work – if people's work is boring, they use travel as a means to 'escape'.

Social class and income

Society can be divided into groups (socio-economic grouping), and as such people from different groups have certain jobs and education, and social characteristics. The higher status groups tend to travel more, take overseas holidays, travel more independently and take more frequent 'short-break' holidays.

Social grade	Social status	Occupation
A	Upper middle class	Higher managerial, professional
B	Middle class	Intermediate managerial, professional
C1	Lower middle class	Supervisory, junior management
C2	Skilled working class	Skilled manual workers
D	Working class	Semi/unskilled
E	Lowest level	Pensioners, casual, unemployed

Figure 3.3: Socio-economic groups

FOR DISCUSSION

Using the socio-economic grouping table, think of different types of holidays and destinations which you think are suitable for each group.

Plan an itinerary for one of the socio-economic groups: include details such as: holiday duration, destination, activities and excursions.

SUMMARY

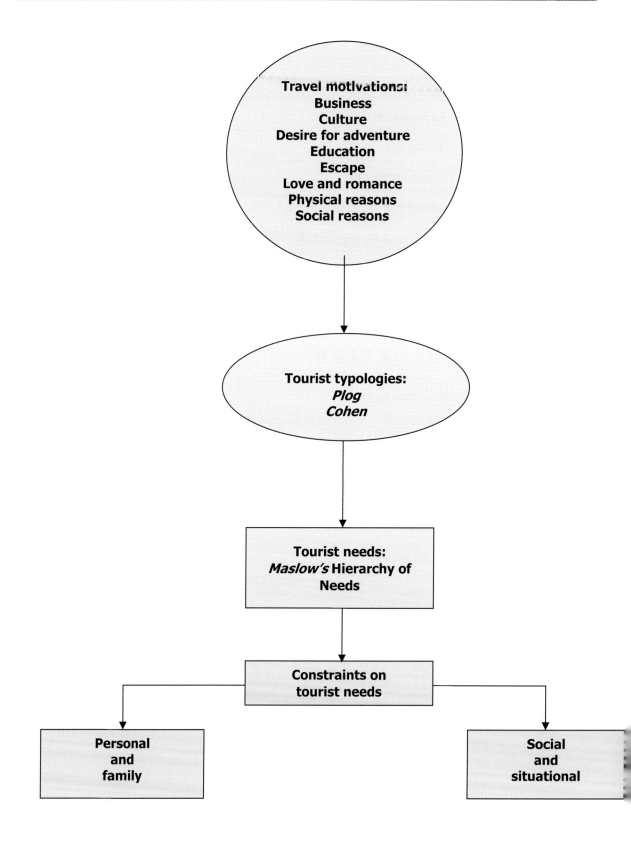

Travel motivations:
Business
Culture
Desire for adventure
Education
Escape
Love and romance
Physical reasons
Social reasons

Tourist typologies:
Plog
Cohen

Tourist needs:
Maslow's Hierarchy of
Needs

Constraints on
tourist needs

Personal
and
family

Social
and
situational

SELF-TEST QUESTIONS

1   Explain what you understand by the terms: Push Factor and Pull Factor.

2   Identify the different travel motivations.

3   What do you understand by the term: MICE tourism.

4   Describe the following terms: sunlust, wanderlust.

5   What does VFR stand for?

6   Identify *Plog's* five different 'tourist typologies'.

7   What are the different levels of *Maslow's* Hierarchy of Needs, and give examples for each need level.

8   Detail the personal and family influences on tourism.

9   Highlight the social and situational influences involved in travel and tourism.

SELF-TEST ANSWERS

1 The 'push factor' is the reason or motivation for travel, for example to relax. The 'pull factor' is the reason why the tourist goes to a specific destination, this can be because it is cheap or they have family living in the destination.

2 Different travel motivations can include: business, culture, desire for adventure, education, escape, love and romance, physical reasons and social reasons.

3 MICE tourism is generally associated with business tourism and stands for: meetings, incentives, conferences and exhibitions.

4 Sunlust is travel undertaken in search of rest and relaxation (R&R), and to enjoy the sun. Wanderlust is when people travel to learn and educate themselves, possibly to learn about a new culture or language.

5 VFR stands for visiting friends and relatives.

6 *Plog's* five tourist types are: allocentric, near-allocentric, mid-centric, near-psychocentric and psychocentric.

7 *Maslow's* Hierarchy of Needs are: Physiological/basic needs, food; safety/security needs, CCTV; social needs, restaurants or bars; esteem needs, a cruise holiday and self-actualisation needs, such as working holidays, for example Kibbutz, Israel.

8 Personal and family influences can include: age, family life cycle, gender and disability.

9 Social and situational influences include: nationality and national identity, tourism and work and social class and income.

ANSWERS TO ACTIVITIES

1 This answer depends on your own experience.

2

People	Holiday	Motivating Factor
1	e	Romance
2	c	Education
3	g	Health
4	f	Social
5	a	Relaxation
6	d	Duty (VFR)
7	h	Wanderlust
8	b	Culture

3 Examples in a tourism context can include:

- **Physiological/Basic needs**: a tent (shelter)
- **Safety/security needs**: Safety deposit boxes, security guards
- **Belonging/Love/Social needs**: hotel bar, restaurants, nightclubs
- **Esteem Needs**: '*keeping-up with the Joneses'*, exotic destinations eg Carribean
- **Self-Actualisation needs**: working holidays, charity work: i-to-i, kibbutz

'Self-actualisation' needs are not related to oneself, they are generally to help others, once all personal needs have been satisfied. These needs can be travel to help others, such as charity work, or some voluntary project work, and examples can include: i-to-i, who provide travel and work to destinations in developing countries, to help in agricultural projects, or teaching English.

Tourist types according to needs:

Maslow Hierarchy of needs	Tourist Type
Physiological/Basic needs	Allocentric – a tourist who requires basic things while visiting a country. They generally require very basic accommodation and local foods, and want to integrate in the local community.
Safety/security needs	Near Allocentric/Mid-centric – tourists who still like adventure, but may require some security when visiting a different country. Their needs may include: safety deposit boxes, while staying in a hostel or a reliable police force during their trip.
Belonging/Love/Social needs	Mid-centric/Psychocentric – tourists who want to meet others during their holiday, and this is generally associated with mass tourism, and package holidays. This can be provided by hotel bars and restaurants, and tour operators; providing entertainment, activities and kids clubs for their guests.
Esteem Needs	Mid-centric/Psychocentric: essentially associated with tourists, who go on organised package holidays, but to destinations that can be regarded as exotic. This can include destinations such as: the Caribbean, the Maldives, places that perhaps not many people, especially from Europe, can afford, therefore it makes them feel superior to the majority of people. Furthermore, it can be regarded as 'keeping up with the Joneses', i.e. going to a place that is similar to your social circles: such as middle-class or those in socio-economic groups: A & B.
Self-Actualisation Needs	Allocentric: these needs, as stated, are generally associated with helping others, as all other needs have been satisfied. These types of tourists are possibly those from higher level socio-economic groups; such as A and Bs, as they desire something different from the normal types of holidays. They perhaps have more than sufficient money, and feel they have to give something back to society, hence voluntary/charity work.

4 Appropriate destinations for each stage can include:

Stage	Destination
Early Childhood	France
Early Teenager	Spain
Young Person	Spain, Dubai
Partnership Stage	Maldives
Family Stage – Early	France, domestic tourism
Family Stage – Late	Spain, Italy
Empty Nest	Cruise holidays, Maldives, Caribbean
Retired	Cruise Holidays, Maldives, Caribbean

CHAPTER 4

DEVELOPMENT OF TOURISM DESTINATIONS AND TRANSPORT AND ACCOMMODATION

Chapter objectives

In this chapter you will learn to

- Investigate the factors required to become a destination
- Identify the six As of a destination
- Determine the concept of destination development

Topic list

The 6 A's of a destination:
Access
Attractions
Accommodation
Activities
Amenities
Ancillary services
Butler's Tourism Area Life Cycle (TALC)

Factors required to become a destination

'The place to which a person is travelling. They can range from purpose-built resorts (eg Sandals Jamaica) or meeting complexes for business travellers (eg Sandton Convention Centre), to specific towns and cities (eg Paris, Prague), to whole regions (eg the Mediterranean, the Cape Winelands) or countries (eg Maldives, The Gambia).'   *Source:* propoortourism.org

"Areas that include a number of individual attractions together with the support services required by tourists."   *Swarbrooke (2002)*

As determined in the last chapter, tourists travel for a number of different reasons, therefore the destination must be prepared to meet the needs of the tourists. To enable us to appreciate and understand the destination in more detail, an amalgam of six As can be applied.

Figure 4.1: The six As of a tourist destination

1 Access

Access involves the movement of tourists from where they live to where they are visiting. Therefore, the overall '**infrastructure**' of a destination is extremely important in enabling the mobility of tourists to a destination, from their home environment.

	**Air**	Air transport is one of the major factors in accessing a destination, especially a destination in a foreign country. It is therefore extremely important that a destination has an airport close by, to facilitate both domestic and international tourist arrivals. This can be a major international 'hub', such as Heathrow, or a regional airport 'spoke', which has regular flights from and to the 'hub' airport.
	**Roads**	Roads and motorways are very important for both domestic and international tourism. In domestic tourism, this may involve travel to a destination from home by car, motorbike or by organised coach tour. In international tourism, roads are very important to enable transfer from the airport to the final destination, by coach transfer (tour operator), taxi, car rental or public transport.
	Ports	Water 'borne' transport also provides another access for tourists travelling to a destination. This can be a 'ferry' which can provide space for travellers with cars, or cruise ships, allowing tourists the opportunity to access the mainland as part of their overall holiday; the cruise.
	**Rail**	Train travel is also very important in accessing destinations for some tourists. Some tourists may use trains for 'day-trips', or to travel to major cities, both domestically and internationally, allowing them to arrive in the centre of the city. The train can also be 'the holiday', with some routes travelling for very long distances, within a particular country or crossing international borders.
	**Disability**	Access, does not only concern access to and from the destination, for more able-bodied persons, it can also relate to persons who are less physically mobile. This can include how transport is adapted to meet these needs of 'disabled' persons, but also how the destination meets these needs, in terms of access to beaches, hotels, parking, and other facilities and attractions.
	Signage	Signage is also extremely important in relation to access. This can include road signs, which enable greater ease to reach a destination or attraction by road, and it can also include signs for pedestrians looking for attractions within cities, or for hikers following a particular 'walking' route.

ACTIVITY 1   20 minutes

In relation to air, road, ports and rail think of some examples of major international 'hub' airports, roads or motorways, ports and rail.

Is access only available to domestic tourists or are these 'access points' attainable by international tourists?

2   Attractions

DEFINITION

Attractions – "generally single units, individual sites or very small, easily delimited geographical areas based on a single key feature".   *Swarbrooke (2002)*

Attractions are very important in a tourist destination; they can provide a 'pull' factor for a destination, therefore a tourist may choose a particular destination over another destination, due to its attractions or because it is an attraction.

Generally, tourist attractions fall into two categories:

- Natural attractions
- Built/man-made attractions

2.1 Natural attractions

Natural attractions are, in many cases, the initial 'pull factor' for many tourist destinations, as tourists want to 'gaze' at beautiful natural attractions, scenery and views that are very different to the environments in which they live and work.

Type of natural attraction	
Beaches	Many tourists, especially 'sunlust' or tourists seeking the 3 Ss (sun, sea and sand), may go to a particular destination because of the beauty of its beaches. The beach may be a feature that has beautiful soft sand, and provide a safe environment for families, alternatively the beach may be aesthetically (visually) beautiful and be the main 'pull' factor for the destination.
Flora and fauna (plant and animals)	Some types of tourism involve visiting places to appreciate the plants and animals. Some 'special-interest' tourists may travel to take photographs of certain species of animals and birds, and plants, or to see them in their natural environments, which may be very different to their home environments.
Lakes	Some people may be attracted to a destination because of the natural feature of lakes. These inland bodies of water can be aesthetically beautiful for some tourists, or they can provide the basis for a range of water-based activities, such as: sailing, canoeing, windsurfing and fishing.
Mountains	These types of natural attractions can again be very pleasing for 'the tourist gaze' and provide a very beautiful environment in which to holiday. Furthermore, mountains provide the basis for a number of 'active' (extreme sports-based) activities, such as: climbing, skiing and walking.
Rivers	Rivers can provide the natural infrastructure for 'water-based' holidays, including 'river-cruises' and boating holidays. They can also provide an attractive setting for water-based activities such as: water-skiing and fishing.
Topography	'The shape and composition of the landscape' *(Dale, 2005)*. The natural scenery itself can be the attraction of a destination. Some people may go to a particular region due to its 'aesthetic beauty', as the landscape is very beautiful to look at, and it provides an 'escape' from their home, possibly urban, environments. In many countries, areas that are aesthetically beautiful are sometimes protected and designated as 'National Parks', or Areas of Outstanding Natural Beauty (AONB), to sustain the area's natural beauty.

A C T I V I T Y   2   3 0   m i n u t e s

Think of an example for each of the types of natural attraction.

Which country is the attraction in?

Which types of tourists do you think go to the destination?

2.2 Factors

Built or man-made attractions generally fall into two categories:

- Built and adapted for visitor purposes
- Built and designed for visitor purposes   *Page & Connell (2006)*

Built attractions adapted for visitor purposes

These are attractions that were not originally designed for visitors, but due to their historical or cultural significance, they have become major tourist attractions. These can include:

- Castles
- Cathedrals
- Historic houses
- Steam railways
- Workplaces

F O R   D I S C U S S I O N

Can you think of any examples of similar 'adapted' tourist attractions in your own region or country?

Have you ever visited these attractions? Why did you visit the attraction?

Purpose-built/attractions designed for visitor purposes

Purpose-built attractions are built to supplement the main attraction, for example a beach. They may also be constructed to attract more tourists to a destination, increasing the 'pull factors'. Some destinations may have few or no natural or built attractions, but due to the benefits tourism can bring, attractions are built to 'entice' tourists to the destination.

Examples of 'purpose-built' attractions can include:

- Galleries
- Leisure centres
- Museums
- Shopping malls
- Theatres
- Theme parks
- Visitor centres
- Water parks
- Wildlife parks and zoos

F O R   D I S C U S S I O N

Think of some examples of 'purpose-built' man-made attractions.

Why do you think these attractions were built?

Temporary attractions

Many destinations hold events or festivals at certain periods of the year, with the intention of attracting visitors to their region. This can include natural and man-made events, such as:

Natural

- The Northern Lights, Norway
- Cherry blossom, Japan

Man-made

- Sports (mega) events: Olympics, football, Grand Prix
- Music festivals: Glastonbury, Mardi Gras (New Orleans), Montreux Jazz Festival (Switzerland)

2.3 Accommodation

Accommodation is extremely important for destinations of all sizes, as some tourists may want to stay overnight, as opposed to excursionists, 'day trippers', who do not require overnight accommodation. Accommodation is of more significance for international tourists, or domestic tourists who have travelled from regions far from the holiday destination.

Depending on the size and dynamic of the destination, there are normally a number of accommodation types available. Generally, accommodation falls into two types:

Catered	Self-catering
Hotels	**Apartments, villas, gites, cottages**
Formal accommodation offering full services. These can include: 'Country House Hotels' with big gardens set in the countryside or a 'Metro Hotel' which can be found in a city centre.	Privately-owned by individuals or companies, where the guests provide their own food and do their own cooking.
Guest houses	**Campus accommodation**
Accommodation for more than six paying guests, with the owner and staff providing more services, for example, dinner.	University halls of residences, where tourists can rent rooms, during non-term time.
Bed and Breakfast (B&B)	**Youth hostel**
Accommodation provided in a private house by the owner for up to six paying guests.	Generally basic accommodation, where guests stay in dormitories or rooms with other people and kitchen facilities are provided.
Farmhouses	**Camp sites**
B&B or Guest House accommodation provided on a working farm.	Privately-owned land, where tourists pay a nightly-fee to pitch their tent or caravan, with washing and electricity sometimes provided.
Other accommodation	
Time-share – tourists pay for access to an apartment for a set date over a number of years.	

In most countries there are different standards of accommodation, and these depend on a number of factors including number of facilities, and standards of quality in a number of areas.

The following table details the hotel grading system in the UK, based on the AA (Automobile Association) accommodation grading standards.

Star rating	Hotel
★	Courteous staff provide an informal yet competent service. The majority of rooms are en suite, and a designated eating area serves breakfast daily and dinner most evenings.
★ ★	All rooms are en suite or have private facilities. A restaurant or dining room serves breakfast daily and dinner most evenings.
★ ★ ★	Staff are smartly and professionally presented. All rooms are en suite, and the restaurant or dining room is open to residents and non-residents.
★ ★ ★ ★	Professional, uniformed staff respond to your needs or requests, and there usually are well-appointed public areas. The restaurant or dining room is open to residents and non-residents, and lunch is available in a designated eating area.
★ ★ ★ ★ ★	Luxurious accommodation and public areas, with a range of extra facilities and a multilingual service available. Guests are greeted at the hotel entrance. High quality menu and wine list.

Figure 4.2: AA accommodation grading standards

FOR DISCUSSION

Do the grading systems operate on a similar system in your own country?

Do you think all destinations have all of these grading ranges from 1 star to 5 stars?

2.4 Activities

During holidays people participate in a number of activities, but these are related to the type of person and essentially the tourist type, therefore the destination has to offer relevant activities to the tourist types that visit the destination.

Activities are generally categorised into two areas:

- **Passive** – activities that are more relaxing
- **Active** – activities that involve some physical exertion

Passive activities	Active activities
Bingo	Golf
Reading books	Watersports
Sightseeing	Walking

Passive activities can be provided by the accommodation, and their 'animation' team, and include 'on-site' activities such as bingo, quizzes, shows and excursions (sightseeing). These activities may be more suitable for those tourists who want to relax on their holiday (rest and relaxation), such as: older tourists or those who are less mobile.

Active activities can be found in some accommodation, such as watersports, organised excursions to go scuba-diving. Within the destination, private companies offer more physical activities enabling the tourist to pick and choose activities as desired. These types of activities are more appropriate for more active tourists, and may include those who are more adventurous, including younger tourists and those more mobile.

FOR DISCUSSION

Can you think of any more examples of active and passive activities?

In relation to the tourist typologies as identified, complete the table with appropriate tourist types for passive activities and active activities?

Passive activities	Tourist type

Active activities	Tourist type

2.5 Amenities (superstructure)

Amenities are the 'extra services' that can be found in the destination to meet the needs of tourists while they are away from their home environment. Due to the large number of people you may find in tourist destinations, both tourists and 'host' populations, the government needs to provide these amenities to 'serve' the permanent and transient populations. The number of amenities will depend on the size of the destination, and some amenities may only be found during the 'peak' or high season, when the populations of some destinations increase substantially.

Examples of amenities include:

- Public toilets
- Signage
- Retail shopping
- Restaurants and cafes
- Visitor centres
- Telecommunications
- Emergency services

ACTIVITY 3   20 minutes

In the table provided list the amenities, including some of your own, and write in the appropriate box if you think they are government (public) or private amenities.

Public amenity	Private amenity

2.6 Ancillary services (support services)

Ancillary services are additional or supplementary services that provide the support needed by the tourist industry. These support services help in the 'multiplier effect' of a tourism destination, and enables more money to be generated and subsequently distributed within the destination and ultimately the host country.

Ancillary services can be both public and private organisations depending on the country, and the larger the destination, the more ancillary services will be found.

Examples of 'ancillary services' include:

- Car hire
- Catering companies
- Entertainment: bars, nightclubs, casinos
- Foreign exchange services
- Insurance
- Laundry services
- Tourism marketing services

ACTIVITY 4   20 minutes

With reference to a destination with which you are familiar, identify the 'ancillary services' within that destination.

How do you think these extra 'support' services help the economy of the destination?

2.7 Butler's Tourism Area Life Cycle (TALC)

To enable an understanding of the development of a tourist destination, a number of concepts have been designed, but the most prominent models of destination development, is the Tourism Area Life Cycle (TALC) *(Butler, 1980)*.

This particular model identifies that destinations go through various stages over time, and in some ways can be compared to the Product Life Cycle (PLC), or your own life cycle.

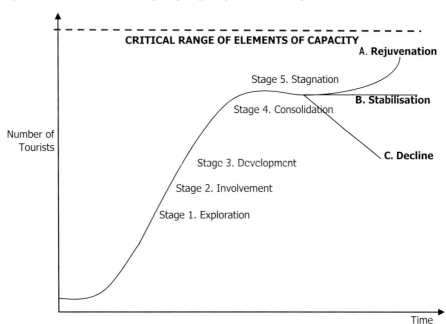

Figure 4.3: Tourism area life cycle (Butler, 1980)

Tourism area life cycle (TALC)

Stage 1 **Exploration**	There are very few tourists (travellers), as not many people know of the destination. These 'travellers', are people who are looking for 'new experience', and travel independently to the destination. The destination has few facilities and basic infrastructure, and the local culture remains and nature is not disturbed.
Stage 2 **Involvement**	There is an increase in tourist numbers and transport links develop. Local people set up new businesses, such as restaurants and offer accommodation in their homes. The public sector investigates tourism development and starts to invest in facilities and infrastructure.
Stage 3 **Development**	The first visitors no longer visit, they discover a new destination. Tourists come on organised tours, and tourist numbers increase rapidly. Private companies move into the area, and the infrastructure and superstructure develops, with lots of construction for tourism. A tourist season has started and there is lots of advertising.
Stage 4 **Consolidation**	The number of tourists is still increasing, but at a slower rate, and the locals begin to resent tourists. The destination is becoming a 'mass tourism' destination, and there is lots of advertising to attract yet more tourists.
Stage 5 **Stagnation**	'Mass tourism'. The carrying capacity of the destination has been reached or even exceeded; the natural environment has been destroyed or displaced by man-made constructions. The destination is over-crowded and over-commercialised.
Rejuvenation	The decision has to be made to take action to redevelop the destination. This would involve lots of money to clean up and possibly re-build the destination.
Stabilisation	The destination may continue as it is, trying to attract lots of tourists and keeping the same infrastructure and superstructure, but this is not sustainable, and eventually many tourists will stop going to the destination.
Decline	The destination becomes very unattractive: tourist facilities close, there is no investment, and tourists numbers to the destination decrease rapidly, tourism may disappear completely.

ACTIVITY 5   20 minutes

Faliraki

Once a tiny fishing village, it is now dubbed 'lively' in brochures. Jet skiing, go-karting, even bungee-jumping are on offer. The beach-front is full of bars and nightclubs, and the noise can be heard several kilometres away. Drinks are six-times the price of the supermarket, and people are trying to get you in to their clubs.

The beach is 'packed' with holiday-makers from morning until dusk, and they leave their mess of fast-food for the seagulls to eat after they leave the beach. The hotel complexes spread from the beach all the way inland, and still more developments are being constructed. Overhead, the next plane can be heard, delivering the next batch of tourists to arrive on their package tour, to experience their 'home from home' in the sun.

What stage of the Butler's TALC is this destination (Faliraki)? Explain why you think it is at this stage?

FOR DISCUSSION

In relation to the TALC, identify which tourist types are appropriate for each stage of the 'life cycle'.

S U M M A R Y

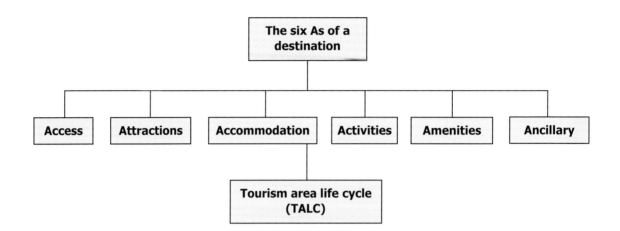

SELF-TEST QUESTIONS

1   What is a destination?

2   Identify the factors of 'access' in relation to a destination.

3   With appropriate examples, identify the two categories of tourist attractions.

4   Provide some examples of temporary attractions.

5   List some examples of catered and self-catering accommodation.

6   Highlight the differences in the grading categories for the hotel sector.

7   Distinguish between 'active' and 'passive' activities, with appropriate examples.

8   Identify some of the public and private sector amenities.

9   What are 'ancillary services' and why are they good for a local or national economy?

10   Identify the different stages of the 'tourism area life cycle', with appropriate examples for each stage.

SELF-TEST ANSWERS

1 A destination is a place to which a person is travelling and includes attractions and support services.

2 Access involves getting to the destination and relates to transport such as air, roads, rail, ports, signage and disabled access.

3 The two categories of tourist attractions are: natural and built or man-made.

4 Temporary attractions can include natural phenomenon, such as the northern lights, and man-made such as: mega-events, for example the football world cup and cultural and music festivals.

5 Catered accommodation includes: guest houses, hotels, bed and breakfasts and farmhouses, self-catered accommodation can include: apartments, chalets, campsites and hostels.

6 The grading for hotels varies from one-star, which provides basic services and facilities up to five-star which includes luxurious accommodation with a lot of services and facilities for guests.

7 Active activities involve some physical exercise and can include: water-sports, mountain-biking, passive activities are more relaxing and include: site-seeing and reading while on holiday.

8 Public sector amenities (superstructure) include: signage, public toilets, shops and visitor centres. Private sector (support) services include: restaurants, cafes and shops.

9 Ancillary services are 'extra' or supplementary services, which are generally privately-owned and include: car hire, catering companies, Foreign exchange services, insurance and marketing services.

10 The different stages of the Tourism Area Life Cycle (TALC) are: Exploration, when there are very few visitors to a destination. Involvement, at this stage tourist numbers increase and locals set up businesses and facilities to meet tourist needs, such as restaurants and providing accommodation. Development, the initial tourists move on to a new destination, and tourist numbers increase rapidly, many private companies, including from outside the area start to operate in the area. Consolidation is when the area is full of tourists, sometimes the number of tourists is greater than the local population, and locals resent the tourists. The area is a mass tourism destination, and is full of the 5A's to accommodate the tourist's needs. Rejuvenation is when investment is put into the area to regenerate the area. Stabilisation is where tourist numbers remain high and tourism dominates in the area. Decline occurs when tourist numbers decline and the quality of facilities and accommodation begins to deteriorate.

ANSWERS TO ACTIVITIES

1 Examples can include:

Airports: Heathrow Airport (London), Frankfurt (Germany), Schipol (Amsterdam, Netherlands), Dubai.

Roads / Motorways: M1 (UK),

Ports: Dover (UK), Calais (France), Rotterdam (Netherlands), Turin (Italy)

Rail: Eurostar (UK, France, Belgium), Palace on Wheels (India), Blue Train (South Africa), Trans-Siberian (Russia)

2

Type of Natural Attraction	Example	Type of tourist
Beaches	Venice Beach, U.S.A. – 'Sunlust'	Psychocentric – package holiday tourists
Flora & Fauna	Serengeti National Park, Tanzania Galapagos Islands, Ecuador	Safari Holidays, Active/Adventure tourists
Lakes	Lake Garda, Italy Lake District, UK	Adventure/Active tourists/ Wanderlust: watersports, hikers, Paintingholidays
Mountains	Himalayas, Nepal	Adventure/Active tourists/ Wanderlust: climbers, gap year/ sabbatical tourists
Rivers	River Rhine, Germany	Active/Passive tourists/Mid-centric – Psychocentric Tourists. Organised river cruises, fishing holidays
Topography	The Alps, France/Switzerland	Active/Passive tourists/Special Interest Tourists (S.I.T.) – Painting holidays, Horse riding Holidays, Hikers, Skiiers

3

Public Amenity	Private Amenity
Public Toilets	Retail shopping
Tourist Information Centre (TIC)	Restaurants and cafes
Emergency Services	
Signage	

4   There is no formal answer to this activity.

5   As we can read from the case study; the resort is described as 'lively', with lots of popular activities, such as jet skiing and go-karting. Furthermore there are lots of bars and nightclubs, and due to this there are some negative impacts such as noise, high prices, litter and lots of construction. From this information and in relation to Butlers Tourism Area Life Cycle (TALC), we can determine that Faliraki is at the 'Stagnation' stage. Therefore, at this point the destination must think about the next stage; should they continue with the destination as it is and possibly let it 'decline' or stabilise, which could be very damaging for the destination's future, or should they decide to 'rejuvenate' the resort, which would involve lots of investment, and sustainable planning, which could be detrimental in the short term?

CHAPTER 5

GOVERNMENTS AND POLITICAL ISSUES

Chapter objectives

In this chapter you will learn to

- Identify the levels of government involvement in tourism
- Understand the role of the different government levels in tourism
- Learn the influence of government within the tourism sector

Topic list

Geographic levels of public sector involvement
Quangos
Regional development agencies

1 Geographic levels of public sector involvement in tourism

"Facilitate, control or limit development... through the provision of basic infrastructure, planning or regulation... activities commonly the responsibility of the public sector with the government at various levels being charged with looking after the public's interest and providing goods and services whose cost cannot be attributed directly to groups or individuals."
Pearce (1989)

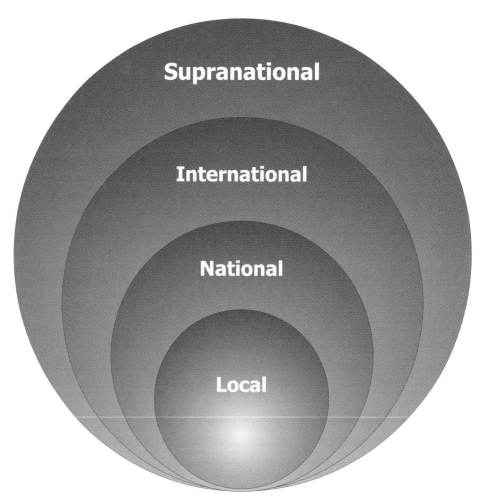

1.1 Supranational organisations

These types of organisations work on an international or regional scale, and involve countries co-operating with each other *"beyond the boundaries of one nation" (Page & Connell, 2006)*, on issues that could influence tourism policy and planning, with *"some significant effect on the international tourism industry" (Page & Connell, 2006)*.

Supranational Organisation

Association of South-East Asian Nations (ASEAN)

 Brunei Darussalam   Cambodia   Indonesia   Laos   Malaysia

 Myanmar   Philippines   Singapore   Thailand   Vietnam

Asia's Perfect 'ten' paradise countries work together to accelerate regional integration in tourism, including the trans-ASEAN transportation network and the Visit ASEAN Campaign and the private sector-led ASEAN Hip-Hop Pass to promote intra-ASEAN tourism.

Asia-Pacific Economic Co-operation (APEC)

APEC consists of 21 member countries, including Asia's Perfect ten paradise countries of ASEAN, and: Australia, Canada, Chile, China, Japan, South Korea, Mexico, New Zealand, Papua New Guinea, Russia and the USA. The 'APEC Tourism Charter' (2000), states "a collective commitment to improve the economic, cultural, social and environmental well-being of APEC member economies through tourism". The Charter establishes four key policy goals:

1. Removal of impediments to tourism business and investment.

2. Increase mobility of visitors and demand for tourism goods and services.

3. Sustainable management of tourism outcomes and impacts.

4. Enhance recognition and understanding of tourism as a vehicle for economic and social development.

European Union (EU)

The European Union consists of 27 member nations, and is very influential in tourism regulation and policy within the region, with 'European Territorial Co-operation Objectives'. This includes 'The Package Travel Directive', joint cross-border tourism strategies, and funding for tourism development projects for member states. Furthermore, there are no travel restrictions and visa requirements within the EU zone for EU citizens.

FOR DISCUSSION

Is your own country a member of any of these 'supranational organisations'?

Can you identify how this 'transnational organisation' helps tourism in your region?

What do you think are the advantages of a country being a member of a 'transnational organisation?

1.2 International tourism organisations

These organisations work on international tourism policy and generally give advice regarding tourism matters.

International tourism organisation		
World Tourism Organisation (UNWTO)		This United Nations (UN) organisation consists of 161 membership countries and territories. The UNWTO helps promote the development of responsible, sustainable and universally accessible tourism, in particular in developing countries.
		The UNWTO 'Global Code of Ethics' for Tourism, ensures member countries, tourist destinations and businesses maximise the positive economic, social and cultural effects of tourism and fully reap its benefits, while minimising its negative social and environmental impacts.
United Nations Educational, Scientific and Cultural Organisation (UNESCO)		UNESCO helps 191 member states prepare their policies, and considers the relationship between tourism and cultural diversity, intercultural dialogue and development. The Organisation tries to minimise poverty, protect the environment and stimulate the mutual appreciation of cultures. UNESCO identifies places of natural and cultural significance '*crucial landmarks for our world*', and designates them as 'World Heritage Sites'.

FOR DISCUSSION

Can you think of any World Heritage Sites?

Why do you think these sites have been designated as World Heritage Sites by UNESCO?

1.3 National tourism organisations (NTO)/national tourist boards (NTB)

Due to the benefits and size of the industry, most national (central) governments have a great interest in tourism. Many national governments have policies and plans for tourism development, which is generally provided by a 'ministry of tourism' or a tourism department; but the extent of government involvement in tourism can differ from country to country.

"Governments have the choice of doing nothing or doing something constructive about tourism policy".

Gunn & Var (2002)

National governments' role in tourism

Co-ordination	Working and sharing information with private tourism organisations, including: ▪ Visitor numbers ▪ Destination Management Systems (DMS), websites
Planning and control	Government planning and control can impact immensely on all organisations, both public and private, involved in tourism, and the functions can involve: ▪ Research and planning for tourism buildings and facilities ▪ Protection and restoration of tourism assets (natural and man-made) ▪ Human resources planning and training

Legislation and regulation	Laws and rules can impact on tourism development indirectly, and examples include: ▪ Visa regulations ▪ Immigration rules ▪ Employment laws Direct rules and legislation can include: ▪ Licences ▪ Accreditations ▪ Planning permission for tourism projects and accommodation
Marketing and promotion	*"Create and protect the brand image of a country/destination."* <div align="right">*Cooper et al. (2005)*</div> The marketing function can include: ▪ Undertaking market research, forecasting trends, collecting and publishing tourism data ▪ Producing and distributing promotional tourism literature ▪ Providing tourist information centres (TIC) and staffing ▪ Promotional and PR activities: domestically and internationally
Social tourism	*"Furtherance of the economically weak or dependent classes of the population."* *Holloway (2006)* In 'social tourism' the state provides: grants, low interest loans or free transport and accommodation for low-income or single-parent families, the elderly, the less-abled or deprived minorities, to maintain the health and well-being of the population. Examples include: Belgium, France and Kyrgyzstan.

Economic	Economic involves the financial functions of the government and this can include:
	
	 ▪ Advice on capital investment and development
	
	 ▪ Government aid for tourism projects
	
	 ▪ Pricing
	    – *Direct* – 'State-owned' attractions, airlines and accommodation
	    – *Indirect* – Foreign exchange restrictions and price controls
	
	 ▪ Taxation: airport departure taxes, ticket taxes, hotel occupancy taxes, local taxes: taxe séjour: France

Safety and security	The safety and security of people is very important for all countries, especially countries that have lots of tourists. If the destination is not safe, possibly due to political unrest or it experiences lots of crime, tourists will not visit, and the destination could miss out on revenue. Therefore, the destination must ensure it has adequate policing and security measures in place, for example in Brazil and Egypt there is a 'tourist police', designated in popular tourist destinations, and in Holland there are tourism victim support services.

FOR DISCUSSION

In relation to the national government involvement as identified above, discuss how your own government influences tourism in your own country, with appropriate examples.

Can you think of any other influences the national government has on tourism in your country?

1.4 Regional government/regional tourist boards (RTB)

Regional governments, funded by national government, are prevalent in most countries throughout the world, and help in the policies and administration of a region. In terms of tourism, most regions have a regional tourist board (RTB), which represents the region at a national level. In general the regional tourist boards functions include:

- Developing strategies in association with local authorities (LAs).
- Encouraging development of tourist amenities and facilities to meet market needs.
- Marketing the region, by producing and supplying literature and activities.

ACTIVITY 1   20 minutes

Investigate your own regional tourist board.

How do they market tourism in the region in which you live?

What tourist amenities and facilities are there in your region?

1.5 Local authorities (LAs)

The third tier or level of government involvement in tourism is that of local authorities (LAs), which work at a local level in developing and representing the interests of a local community, often between the public, private and voluntary bodies involved in tourism at a local level.

Typical objectives of the local authority include:

- Creating or improving the image of the area as a destination
- Extending visitor stays
- Increasing and upgrading local attractions
- Increasing visitor numbers
- Increasing visitor spend
- Stimulating private-sector involvement in tourism   *Holloway (2006)*

To realise these objectives, the LAs have a number of responsibilities in relation to tourism in their local area. This can include:

- Car and coach parking
- Health, hygiene and safety, including: litter disposal, public toilets
- Leisure facilities – for tourists and residents, including: sports centres, parks, theatres, museums, conference centres and so on
- Maintaining local historic buildings
- Marketing and promoting the local area
- Planning (town and country planning) within the local area
- Power controls over land use
- Preservation and conservation of the local environment
- Signs to local attractions and places of interest
- Tourism statistics and data, which is then supplied to regional tourist boards
- Tourist information centres (TIC)

ACTIVITY 2   **2 0   m i n u t e s**

Visit your local tourist information centre, and collect some information regarding the local tourist attractions within your area. Which of these attractions do you think are private, and which are run and owned by the local authority?

2   Quangos

Some agencies work in a particular geographical area or on a particular project, *ad hoc*. These agencies must put into practice government policy, either national or regional, but have the flexibility to manage their own affairs. These *quangos* (Quasi-Autonomous Non-Governmental Organisations), which can be national tourism organisations or national tourist boards, have grown in number since the 1980s, and are very common in the UK and other western nations.

3   Regional development agencies (RDA)

In England, RDAs were set up in different regions to stimulate and promote investment into the region. Receiving money from the Department for Culture, Media and Sports (DCMS), the government department responsible for tourism in the UK, one of the regional development agencies main tasks is to develop economic strategies for tourism within a region, by attracting private investment and subsequently stimulating the economy – 'economic multiplier effect'.

FOR DISCUSSION

Do you have any *quangos* or regional development agencies operating within the area where you live? If so, what do they do?

S U M M A R Y

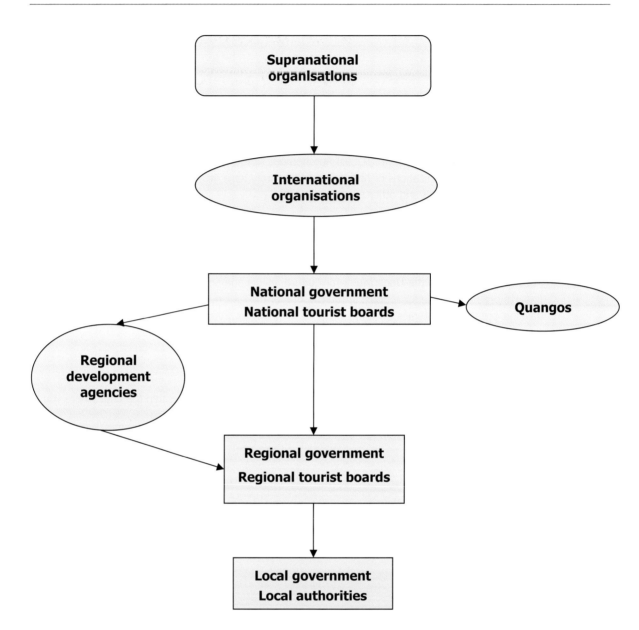

SELF-TEST QUESTIONS

1 Name some examples of supranational organisations.

2 State some advantages and disadvantages of supranational organisations.

3 UNESCO and the UNWTO are two examples of international organisations. Explain their functions in relation to tourism.

4 What are some of the functions of national governments in relation to tourism?

5 What does NTB stand for and name some of its primary roles?

6 Regional tourist boards (RTB) play an important part in tourism. Name some of the functions of a RTB.

7 Name some of the responsibilities of a local authority (LA).

8 What is a quango?

9 What is the role of a RDA?

SELF-TEST ANSWERS

1 Some examples of supranational organisations, include: Asean, APEC and the EU.

2 Some advantages of supranational organisations are: economic benefits of investment, easier access for visitors from within the region and unification of the area. Disadvantages can include imbalances in investment, confrontation and disagreements among member states.

3 UNESCO prepare policies, and considers the relationship between tourism and cultural diversity, intercultural dialogue and development. The organisation tries to minimise poverty, protect the environment and stimulate the mutual appreciation of cultures. UNESCO identifies places of natural and cultural significance 'crucial landmarks for our world', and designates them as 'World Heritage Sites'.

WTO helps promote the development of responsible, sustainable and universally accessible tourism, in particular in developing countries. The 'Global Code of Ethics' for tourism, ensures member countries, tourist destinations and businesses maximise the positive economic, social and cultural effects of tourism and fully reap its benefits, while minimising its negative social and environmental impacts.

4 Functions of national governments in relation to tourism, are: co-ordination, planning and control legislation and regulation, marketing and promotion, social tourism, economic, safety and security.

5 NTB stand for National Tourist Board and its role includes: developing strategies in association with local authorities. Encouraging development of tourist amenities and facilities to meet market needs, on a national level.

6 The functions of the RTB are to develop strategies in association with NTBs and encourage development of tourist amenities and facilities to meet market needs, on a regional level.

7 Local authorities role involves: creating or improving the image of the area as a destination, extending visitor stays, increasing and upgrading local attractions, increasing visitor numbers and spend, and stimulating private-sector involvement in tourism.

8 A quango is a Quasi-Autonomous Non-Governmental Organisation and it is set up by governments to deal with a particular project.

9 A regional development agency's main tasks are to develop economic strategies for tourism within a region, by attracting private investment and subsequently stimulating the economy within the region, 'Economic Multiplier Effect'.

ANSWERS TO ACTIVITIES

The activities in this chapter involve personal research, so there are no formal answers provided.

CHAPTER 6

POSITIVE AND NEGATIVE IMPACTS OF TOURISM

Chapter objectives

In this chapter you will

- Identify the positive and negative impacts of tourism
- Interpret the economic impacts of tourism
- Learn the environmental impacts of tourism
- Investigate the socio-cultural impacts of tourism

Tourism is a huge industry, "*probably the single most important industry in the world*" *(Holloway, 2006)* and due to its size and nature 'labour intensive', it employs "*127 million people around the world*" *(Holloway, 2006)*, although some figures suggest it employs around "*207 million jobs*" *(Page & Connell, 2006)*. Many countries, in particular developing countries, turn to tourism as a way of generating income, due to the abundance of benefits tourism can bring. But, the rewards are sometimes negated by the negative impacts of the development of the industry.

This chapter will look at those positive and negative impacts of tourism, in relation to economic, environmental and socio-cultural factors.

1 The economic impacts of tourism

As stated, tourism is a huge industry, and with it, there are some very attractive economic benefits: "*in 2004, worldwide tourism receipts, excluding international fares, reached $622 billion.*" (WTO), and accounts for "11% of gross domestic product" (WTTC), therefore, many countries, in particular developing countries are constantly looking at tourism as way to generate their economies. Furthermore, it is becoming cheaper and easier for people to travel and the increasing wealth of some of the largest nations on earth, most notably China and India, is making tourism an even more attractive proposition for economic growth.

Figure 6.1: The positive and negative economic impacts of tourism

1.1 The positive economic impacts of tourism

Positive economic impacts of tourism	
Balance of payments	"*The quantity of a country's own currency flowing out of the country minus the amount flowing in*". *http://economics.about.com* Tourism is a good industry to reduce or minimise a country's balance of payments. Tourists bring the destination currency into the receiving country (exchanged in the overseas country), or they exchange their own currency in the destination. This means that the money spent by the tourist in the destination is 'credited' to the receiving country's economy, and 'debited' from the tourist's own country, meaning that the host country is receiving more money from outside its borders. This is extremely beneficial for countries receiving tourists from 'high value' currency countries, such as the European Union zone, the United States and the United Kingdom.
Employment	Tourism is beneficial for creating jobs, and three types of job creation can be attributed to tourism: - **Direct employment** – these are jobs directly involved in tourism, for example in a hotel or a tourist attraction. - **Indirect employment** – jobs created in the tourism supply sector, for example a catering company providing meals to an airline. - **Induced employment** – these are jobs created due to increased wealth of the locals from tourism, and the locals spending more money in their local economy.
Income	Tourism creates money in a destination's local economy, through: - **Wages and salaries** – from the locals' employment in the local area (directly, indirectly or induced). - **Profits** – with local businesses making money from the tourists. - **Rent** – from leasing accommodation to tourists and 'migrating' workforce. - **Tax** – the 'public purse' also benefits from tourist expenditure, in the form of taxes, either a local tax or a national tax, such as value added tax (VAT), which can then go towards further investment in the local or national economy.
Investment and Development	Investment and development, can be from the 'public' sector (government) or from private sector. **Public** – The government may want to develop the area, by investing in the infrastructure and superstructure of a destination, to make it more accessible and attractive for tourism. This may mean the construction of new roads, airports and telecommunications. **Private** – Many companies, in particular multinational companies (MNCs), may see the area as being an attractive place to set up some operations. This in turn can lead to further investment from other 'large' organisations investing in the area – 'multiplier effect'.

Positive economic impacts of tourism

Multiplier effect   Tourism can have many positive 'knock-on' effects, 'the multiplier effect', meaning that "*tourist expenditure will inject additional cash flow into the regional economy and increase regional income*"

Page & Connell (2006)

- **Employment multiplier** – further jobs (indirect and induced) are created by direct tourism employment.

- **Income multiplier** – additional income is created in an economy as a result of direct tourist expenditure. The locals have more money from the employment multiplier, which they in turn, spend in the local economy in shops, supermarkets etc.

"The money spent by tourists in the area will be re-spent by recipients (other businesses and locals) in the area."

Holloway (2006)

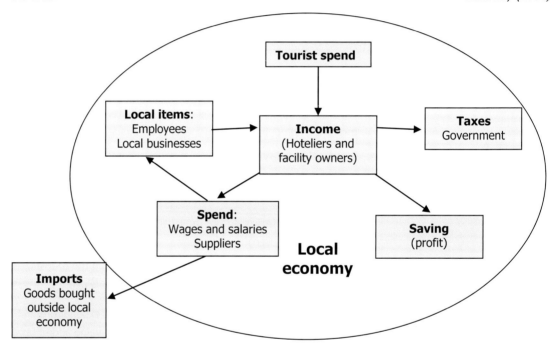

Figure 6.2: Effect of tourist spend on the local economy

Tourist spend – money is directly spent by the tourist on the holiday.

Income – the tourist's money is received by hotel and facility owners.

Taxes – the hoteliers and facility owners have to pay government taxes, such as council tax, corporation taxes to the government, of which some will be local and some will be national.

Saving – some of the money received by the proprietors of facilities and hotels will be kept as profit.

Spend – the owners of the businesses that receive the money **(income)** will need to spend some on wages and salaries and some on supplies **(stock)**, within the local economy or outside the local area **(imports)**.

Local items – employees and locals will then spend their wages in the local shops, such as supermarkets.

Money further circulates in the economy; locals spend money in local shops, which means local shopkeepers need to buy supplies and so on. Therefore the initial money spent in the area has multiplied as it has entered other areas of the local economy.

ACTIVITY 1   20 minutes

The government has decided to build a new airport in your region, so it can try to expand tourism in the area.

Write a list of the other types of companies or industries that would be attracted or would be needed in the area near to the airport.

1.2 The negative economic impacts of tourism

Negative economic impact of tourism	
Dependency	Some countries are 'economically dependent' on tourism, especially some less developed countries, which may have few other industries. Therefore, if tourism is lost or decreases in that country (credit crunch, natural disasters or political instability), a lot of income could be lost and impact hugely on the national economy, in terms of loss of revenue, balance of payments and taxes.
Inflation	Generally with increased demand comes increased inflation, which means that the prices and values of land and products, increases. Locals may not be able to continue to afford to live and invest in businesses in the area, which in turn could lead to negative socio-cultural impacts of tourism.
Leakages	*"Money that drops out of circulation within a local economy, by being saved or spent on goods and services outside the economy."* *Cooper et al. (2005)* Tourism may attract a lot of investment, but in many cases the investment is from companies outside the borders of the receiving country 'multinational companies' (MNCs). Many of these MNCs, have their headquarters (HQs) in different countries, therefore the profit made from the tourist activity does not stay in the host destination, it goes back to the country of residence of the company's HQ. Leakage can also occur when a country or destination has to purchase items from outside the economy 'import' (national or local). This is a particular issue for small island states, which have to 'buy-in' goods to satisfy the tastes and needs of tourists from more larger, developed nations, especially 'psycho-centric tourists'.
Opportunity costs (displacement effect)	*"developing tourism at the expense of other activities or areas of investment."* *Page & Connell (2006)* This is money (public) that if invested in tourism, is not available for other uses. Local communities could lose out on facilities and infrastructure that they need. A 'cost-benefit analysis' can be performed to determine the best way to invest the money, but in many cases the local population's needs are neglected.

FOR DISCUSSION

Think about the tourist areas in your region.

Are the prices of goods more expensive in the tourist area compared to where you live?

Are there any big hotels and fast-food places in the tourist area? What are the names of these hotels and fast-food restaurants? Are any of the hotels and fast-food restaurants locally-owned?

2   Environmental impacts of tourism

'The environment, natural and artificial, is the most important factor of the tourism product.'

Cooper et al. (2005)

In recent years, and in particular since the United Nations (UN) Conference on the Environment and Development (1992) also known as the Rio Earth Summit, there has been an increased interest in the environment and the impacts that human development and interaction has on it. This is it particularly true with tourism and many tourism stakeholders are increasingly respecting the environmental impacts of tourism.

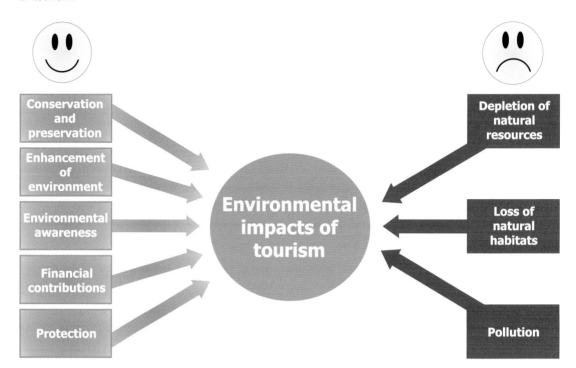

Figure 6.3: Environmental impacts of tourism

2.1   Positive environmental impacts of tourism

Positive environmental impacts of tourism	
Conservation and preservation	Tourism can help to conserve natural environments, by the designation or 'zoning' of natural areas. In many countries 'National Parks' have been established, with very strict regulations on development, and rules for visitors.
	Preservation of built or man-made constructions, for example castles or places of worship, such as cathedrals or mosques, can also be achieved through tourism. Visitors may be allowed to visit these 'built attractions', but many areas of the attractions may be 'zoned-off' with restricted access. Money raised from visitors can help in restoring and maintaining these important 'man-made' sites.
Enhancement of environment	In some areas, tourism can help the environment aesthetically (visually), by making a place look better. This can involve the cleaning of areas, through money generated from tourism, reforestation, planting trees to balance tourism development, or projects designed to make a more pleasant environment such as public art or public squares. An example of this is London, where the Olympic Games of 2012 will lead to the creation of a huge public park for residents and visitors to enjoy.

Positive environmental impacts of tourism	
Environmental awareness	In recent years and since the Rio Earth Summit there has been an increase in public appreciation of the environment and awareness of environmental problems. More tourism and hospitality organisations, both public and private, are adapting and informing consumers of environmental issues, this includes hotels giving guidelines on laundry and keys that activate the electricity in rooms. Many tour operators are adapting products to meet the needs of the increasing care for the environment, by incorporating and providing information to tourists of the environmental consequences of their actions.
Financial contributions	Direct financial contributions – revenue from park-entrance fees and similar sources can be allocated specifically to pay for the protection and management of environmentally sensitive areas. Contributions to government revenues – user fees, income taxes, taxes on sales or rental of recreation equipment, and licence fees for activities such as hunting and fishing can provide the funds needed to manage natural resources. These monies can be used for overall conservation programmes and activities, such as park ranger salaries and park maintenance.
Protection	Environmental protection, conservation and restoration of biological diversity and sustainable use of natural resources, can be achieved through tourism, in particular from government environmental management and planning, which can help prevent deterioration of the environment. Cleaner production techniques, such as green building (energy-efficient and non-polluting construction materials, sewage systems and energy sources) and waste treatment and disposal are often major, long-term environmental problems in the tourism industry, pollution prevention and waste minimisation techniques are especially important.

2.2 Negative environmental impacts of tourism

Negative environmental impacts of tourism	
Depletion of natural resources	Tourism can have a hugely negative impact on the natural resources of the receiving region, this can include depletion of:
	Water resources: the overuse of water for hotels, swimming pools, golf courses and personal use of water by tourists, can lead to shortages of water and may mean that the 'host' population may not have enough water for their own needs, as in some areas tourists are the priority. "*Tourists consume more water when on holiday than they do at home, the amount used can run up to 440 litres a day, almost double what the inhabitants of an average Spanish city use. An average golf course in a tropical country such as Thailand needs 1500kg of chemical fertilisers, pesticides and herbicides per year and uses as much water as 60,000 rural villagers.*" *Tourism Concern*
	Local resources: energy, food and other raw materials, are excessively used in tourism for building and transport of these resources (vehicles adding to congestion), as tourists have a high demand for heating, hot water, etc and extraction of raw materials impacts on the physical impression of a destination. Many areas also suffer from overcrowding in high season: "*some destinations have ten times more inhabitants in the high season as in the low season*". *Tourism Concern*

Negative environmental impacts of tourism

	Land degradation: due to the activities of tourism, land can be destroyed. Construction of tourism and hospitality facilities and infrastructure devastates beautiful natural areas such as forests. Tourist activities can also have a big impact on the land and vegetation; walking, skiing, and more 'active' activities can lead to deforestation and erosion of grasslands.
Loss of habitats	*On land* (terrain): animals and plants (flora and fauna), can be displaced and lose their habitats due to the activities and construction of tourism infrastructure and superstructure. The building of hotels and tourism facilities destroys the animals' environment and natural vegetation. *Offshore* (water-based): activities in the sea, such as marina development, construction of breakwaters and water-based activities can destroy the marine wildlife. Coral reefs are suffering worldwide from reef-based tourism developments, increased sediments in the water, trampling by tourists and divers, ship groundings, pollution from sewage, over-fishing, and fishing with poisons and explosives. *"In the Philippines and the Maldives, dynamiting and mining of coral for resort building materials has damaged fragile coral reefs and depleted the fisheries that sustain local people and attract tourists."* www.gdrc.org.uk
Pollution	*Air:* tourism obviously involves travel and the majority of travel involves using some sort of transport. *"Tourism now accounts for more than 60% of air travel"* (www.bd-experts.com). Buses, cars and coaches, are very common forms of tourist transport, and all significantly contribute to carbon dioxide (CO_2) emissions, not only on a local, but on a global scale. *Noise:* tourist transport and activities all contribute to noise pollution. Traffic noise from aeroplanes, buses, cars and coaches and tourist activities such as: entertainment (bars and nightclubs), jet-skiing and snow-mobiles all contribute, which can negatively impact on the tourist experience (rest and relaxation), and also disturb animal (fauna) habitats. *Visual* (aesthetic): with large numbers of tourists in an area, solid waste and littering is a problem. Improper disposal of waste can visually pollute beaches, rivers, natural scenic and urban areas. "*Some trails in the Peruvian Andes and in Nepal, frequently visited by tourists, have been nicknamed "Coca-Cola trail" and "toilet paper trail"*. (www.gdrc.org.uk) Tourism constructions (infrastructure and superstructure): such as hotels and tourist facilities, often do not complement the nature and architecture of a destination, and these 'eyesores' or 'blots on the landscape', can add to the visual or aesthetic pollution of a destination. *Water:* Tourist activities, transport and waste disposal in popular tourist destinations contribute seriously to the contamination of water in these areas. Water-based transport such as cruise ships and boats emit waste into the sea. "*The Caribbean region, stretching from Florida to French Guiana, receives 63,000 port calls from ships each year, and they generate 82,000 tons of garbage. On average, passengers on a cruise ship each account for 3.5 kilograms of garbage daily."* (Our Planet, UNEP, 1999) Sewage pollution and run-off from hotels, recreation and other facilities leads to polluted seas and lakes surrounding tourist attractions, damaging the flora and fauna, and also threatening the health of humans.

FOR DISCUSSION

Tourism has some positive environmental impacts, can you think of any examples in the region where you live.

What different ways can the negative environmental impacts of tourism be overcome or minimised?

3 Socio-cultural impacts of tourism

Tourism – *"the activities of persons travelling to and staying in places outside their usual environment..."* *(UNWTO, 1993)*

DEFINITION

As the definitions of tourism identify, tourism is mainly concerned with the visitors to destinations, but tourism also has huge impacts, both positively and negatively, on the 'host' or 'receiving' populations.

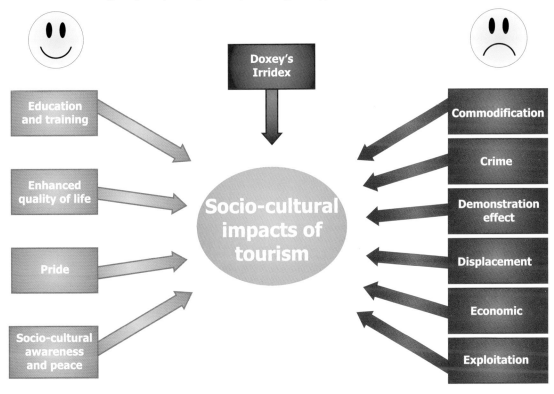

Figure 6.4: Socio-cultural impacts of tourism

3.1 Positive socio-cultural impacts of tourism

Positive socio-cultural impacts of tourism	
Education and training	Tourism can provide the opportunity for locals to learn new skills and qualifications, which are essential to work in the tourism and travel industry. This may include tour operators and major hotel organisations training and educating staff in the areas of: customer service and IT, which are essential for dealing with international customers and reservations and ticketing.
Enhanced quality of life	As we have seen, the positive economic impacts of tourism are extremely attractive, including investment and increasing the income of locals. Investment can help to improve the local infrastructure and superstructure: roads, sanitation, shops and facilities, which can all be used by locals. Furthermore, increasing incomes from locally-owned businesses and more local jobs means that the 'host' population may have more money to spend (disposable income).
Pride	With an increase in visitors and investment comes an increase in 'local pride'. Many tourists want to 'see' the local culture of the receiving destination, and this can include experiencing the local ceremonies, rituals and skills and crafts. This can give the 'host' population a renewed interest in their own heritage and traditions and make them feel proud of their own culture.
Socio-cultural awareness and peace	Tourism enables people from different cultures to meet and gain a greater knowledge through personal exchange and interaction. This 'first hand' cultural exchange education can create a greater understanding of other cultures, both on the part of the receiving population and the generating populations, in terms of beliefs, customs, language and religion.

3.2 Negative socio-cultural impacts of tourism

Negative socio-cultural impacts of tourism	
Commodification	'Commodification' is concerned with the ceremonies, cultural performances and rituals "*being changed to suit the needs and wishes of tourists*" *(Cooper et al., 2005)*. These performances and ceremonies are made more colourful and dramatic to attract the tourists – "*culture becomes a commodity for financial transactions*" *(Cooper et al., 2005)* – and do not really show the 'true' culture of the destination – 'staged authenticity'.
Crime	Crime is common in many destinations with high numbers of tourists. Tourists obviously go on holiday with substantial amounts of money, and take with them valuables such as digital cameras and mp3 players. Some of the indigenous population may not be able to afford these items and see the tourists as an easy target, in an unfamiliar environment. Furthermore, some visitors on holiday may want to have experiences very different than they would in their usual environments. This may mean illegal experiences such as taking drugs and prostitution ('sex tourism'), therefore some people take advantage of this, in exchange for financial gain.

Negative socio-cultural impacts of tourism	
Demonstration effect	"*Changes in attitudes, values or behaviour which can result from merely observing tourists*" *(De Kadt, 1979)*. The host population see the tourists' behaviour, clothes and possessions and try to emulate (copy) them. This can lead to a loss of identity of the local culture, in particular among the younger population, who turn to more 'western' styles of clothes and music ('westernisation').
Displacement	The potential economic benefits of tourism, leads to the development of tourism infrastructure and superstructure. These constructions often mean that large areas of land are needed, and this can often be land where the indigenous population live, "*local people being moved away from their place of residence to make way for tourism development have been recorded*" *(Page & Connell, 2006)*.
Economic	Tourism can have a huge economic impact on a destination, and in turn on the local population. It can lead to increased prosperity of the local population, which can cause social tensions between incoming migrants looking for work, and the host population. Furthermore, with the increasing popularity of a destination and the resources needed to support the industry, prices, for example of housing due to second home ownership and taxes may increase, putting greater financial pressure on the local population, again causing resentment.
Exploitation	Tourism may create jobs for a destination, but sometimes these jobs are not as attractive as they may initially seem, with some organisations exploiting the local population for their own benefit. Child labour, forced labour and lower level jobs for locals, are some examples of how organisations, including some 'globalised' companies, are reaping the economic benefits of tourism for their own advantage.

4 *Doxey's* Irritation Index (Irridex) (1975)

This index was designed to measure a host population's perception of tourists with the development of the destination over time.

Euphoria area	'Euphoria' relates to the early stages of *Butler's* 'Tourism Area Life Cycle' (TALC), where the destination has few visitors and little development has taken place. At this stage the 'receiving' population are very happy that the tourists are visiting the area, and welcome them, with informal relationships established between the visitors and the locals.
Apathy	As the destination becomes more developed and the visitor numbers increase the relationship between the visitors and locals becomes more formal, visitors are taken for granted, and are only seen as a source of money.
Annoyance	The destination has developed to 'saturation' point, with the number of tourism developments and tourist numbers so much that the local population is very annoyed with the whole of the tourism industry within their region.
Antagonism	The destination has reached a point of development where there are many negative impacts, and the hosts openly express their feelings to the visitors, blaming them for all the negative impacts.

Doxey (1975)

S U M M A R Y

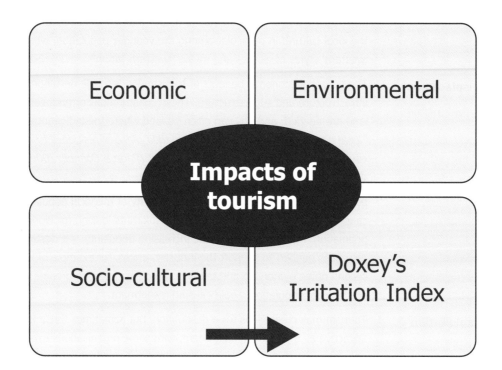

SELF-TEST QUESTIONS

1   Identify and explain some of the positive economic impacts of tourism.

2   What does TIM stand for?

3   Explain the TIM model.

4   Identify the negative economic impacts of tourism.

5   How can tourism benefit the environment of a destination?

6   What negative impacts does tourism have on the environment?

7   Explain the positive socio-cultural impacts of tourism.

8   What negative socio-cultural impacts can tourism have on a destination?

9   Identify and explain the stages of *Doxey's* Irritation Index (Irridex).

SELF-TEST ANSWERS

1 Some of the positive economic impacts of tourism include: balance of payments, investment and development, employment, income and the tourism income multiplier.

2 TIM stands for tourism income multiplier and involves the money spent by tourists in an area will be re-spent by recipients (other businesses and locals) in the area.

3 As stated by *Holloway (2006)*, the Tourism Income Multiplier (TIM) is *"the money spent by tourists in the area which will be re-spent by recipients (other businesses and locals) in the area".*

The money tourists spend in the area is received (income) by local hotel and business owners, such as shops, bars and restaurants. Once this money is received by proprietors it is distributed into many different areas of the local economy, in the form of **taxes**: such as local council taxes, **spending:** the owners need to pay staff wages and salaries, which in turn is spent in the local economy by employees, ie rent or mortgages for accommodation, and in local shops and supermarkets. Furthermore, the owners of local businesses have to replace the goods they have sold therefore they need to purchase extra stock and items, which invariably they purchase from local suppliers, such as wholesalers located in the local area.

On occasions some of the money spent by tourists does not enter the local economy. Some of the tourist's income has to pay for national taxes, such as Value Added Taxes (VAT) and national insurance, moreover some of the income is retained and saved by the local business owners. Finally, due to the global nature of the industry, many tourism and hospitality organisations are '**multi-national companies**' (MNC), and they have their headquarters in countries outside of the borders where the money is received (**leakages**), therefore the profits go to the country where the **MNC** is based, thus it escapes from the economy where the money is received.

4 Negative economic impacts of tourism are leakages, opportunity costs, inflation and dependency on tourism.

5 Tourism can help to conserve and preserve natural and built environments, including forests and areas of natural beauty and look after old and culturally significant buildings such as castles, cathedrals and monuments.

6 Negative impacts of tourism on the environment can include: depletion of natural resources, loss of natural habitats and pollution.

7 Positive socio-cultural impacts of tourism involve education and training, enhanced quality of life, pride of locals and awareness and peace.

8 Negative socio-cultural impacts on a destination can include: commodification, crime, demonstration effect, displacement of people, economic factors and exploitation of the host population.

9 *Doxey's* Irritation Index (Irridex) involves the following: euphoria, when the local population is very pleased to meet tourists. Apathy, the locals just see the tourists as an economic income. Annoyance, where the locals are not happy with the tourists, possibly because there are too many. Antagonism, where the 'host' population show the tourists their displeasure.

ANSWER TO ACTIVITY

1 Other companies or industries that would be attracted or would be needed in the area near to the airport can include:

- Hotels
- Catering companies
- Petrol companies
- Ancillary services such as: car hire, taxi companies
- Shopping centres
- Restaurants
- Conference centres
- Cleaning companies

CHAPTER 7

TOURISM ETHICS AND SUSTAINABLE TOURISM

Chapter objectives

In this chapter you will

- Be introduced to sustainable tourism
- Learn sustainable tourism policies and procedures
- Investigate best tourism practices
- Identify the codes of conduct for ethical tourism

Topic list

The rise of environmental concern

Sustainable tourism

Sustainability tools

Sustainable tourism guidelines and principles

The World Tourism Organisation's Global Code of Ethics for Tourism

In recent years there has been a greater emphasis on 'ethical' business, possibly due to the economic growth of some countries and increased globalisation, and various organisations have been established to deal with 'unethical' business practices.

This is the same in the tourism industry, which has grown extremely quickly over the last 50 years. "*From 1950 to 2005, international tourism arrivals expanded at an annual rate of 6.5%, growing from 25 million to 806 million travellers*" (www.unwto.org), and as forecasts predict this is set to further increase "*by 2020 international arrivals are expected to surpass 1.5 billion people*" (www.unwto.org). In particular, many developing nations are looking at the benefits of tourism, and are trying to increase tourism within their borders. But as we have identified, the benefits of tourism do come with problems, and in recent years a number of organisations and policies in the sector have been established, perhaps due to increased awareness, to deal with these negative and sometimes 'unethical' problems.

1 The rise of environmental concern

The rise in environmental awareness and green issues is not a new phenomenon. The Greeks wrote about the earth as "*a living goddess*" *(Page & Connell, 2006)* and all throughout history from the Romans to the Arcadian or Eco-centric view of the 18th Century, the environment has been of great concern for humans. But it wasn't until the 1970s that international debate on environmental issues really began.

Year	
1972	**United Nations Conference on the Human Environment (Stockholm)** 119 countries met to discuss environmental problems
1980	**International Union for the Conservation of Nature and Natural Resources (IUCN)** World conservation strategy to promote sustainable development
1984	**The World Commission on Environment and Development** Established to put forward proposals for environmental development changes and action
1987	**'Our Common Future' (The Brundtland Report)** Investigated objectives for future economic growth and the environment and defined sustainable development: "development that meets the needs of the present without compromising the needs of future generations" (1987-9)
1992	**UN conference on Environment and Development 'The Rio Earth Summit'** Established 'Agenda 21' strategy
2000	**United Nations Environmental Programme (UNEP)** Initiative for Sustainable Tourism
2002	**World Summit on Sustainable Development (Johannesburg)** Looked at the importance of tourism sustainability

2 Sustainable tourism

"*...meets the needs of present tourists and host regions while protecting and enhancing opportunity for the future. It is envisaged as leading to management of all resources in such a way that economic, social, and aesthetic needs can be fulfilled while maintaining cultural integrity, essential ecological processes, and biological diversity, and life support systems.*"
UNWTO (1987)

"*Tourism which is economically viable but does not destroy the resources in which the future of tourism will depend, notably the physical environment and the social fabric of the host community.*"
Swarbrooke (1999)

"*Sustainability principles refer to the environmental, economic, and socio-cultural aspects of tourism development, and a suitable balance must be established between these three dimensions to guarantee its long-term sustainability.*"
UNWTO (2004)

Principles of sustainable tourism

Socio-cultural

Respect authenticity of host communities, conserve their built and living cultural heritage and traditional values, and contribute to inter-cultural understanding and tolerance

Environment

Make optimal use of environmental resources, maintaining ecological processes and help conserve natural heritage and biodiversity

Economic

Ensure viable, long-term economic operations, providing socio-economic benefits to all stakeholders that are fairly distributed, including stable employment and income-earning opportunities and social services to host communities, and contributing to poverty alleviation.

Sustainable tourism

UNWTO (2004)

3 Sustainability tools

Agenda 21	*'an action plan for sustainable development'*. Established at the 'Rio Earth Summit' (1992), this plan commits governments to consider the environment and development, including elements of tourism activities such as: accommodation, entrepreneurship, food, transport and waste management, many of which occur at local level 'Local Agenda 21'.
Carrying capacity	There are four types of carrying capacity: **Ecological**: a measure of the number of people that can be accommodated on a site before damage occurs to the environment. **Economic**: the number of people that can visit a place before the economy of the destination is negatively affected. **Perceptual**: the number of people that can be accommodated on a site before the visitor experience is damaged. **Physical carrying capacity**: this is a measurement of the number of tourists (people) that can be physically accommodated on a site.
Corporate environmental management	Many organisations are following strict policies to ensure they are respecting the environment, this includes the 'ISO14000/140001' and British Standards Institute 'BS7750'. In tourism many tour operators have joined the 'Tour Operator Initiative' (2000), which involves the companies setting performance indicators and submitting sustainability reports on a yearly basis.
Environmental auditing	This enables companies to audit their own business practice, in the UK. 'The Green Audit Kit' concentrates on: energy, health, local environment, purchasing, transport and waste.
Environmental impact assessment (EIA)	This considers the environmental impact of a development from start to finish, and from this assessment a decision will be made if the project should be approved or if more other environmental management procedures should be added. In tourism an EIA may be carried out on developments such as: holiday villages, marinas and ski resorts.

BPP
LEARNING MEDIA

Environmental policies and statements	Many organisations, both public and private, have developed their own policies and statements on their environmental performance. This includes many airlines (British Airways, EasyJet) which produce statements and reports informing of their 'clean and green' credentials, and many tour operators, which have areas of their web sites dedicated to their environmental 'green' practices, including TUI (Thomson), and Thomas Cook.
Visitor management	*'aims to protect the environment while providing visitor enjoyment,'* and can be performed in relation to three areas: **Control volume**: this can include limiting visitor numbers, encouraging people to visit at different times, or visiting alternative locations. **Modify behaviour**: this attempts to adapt the behaviour of visitors through providing information 'codes of conduct' and marketing material, guided walks and signs. Education can also be a useful technique, combining a visitor centre with education. **Adapt a resource**: this can include hardening footpaths, and constructing purpose-built facilities. *Grant (1994)* identifies **'hard measures'**, physical and financial restrictions, such as: parking and entrance fees and 'zoning'; and **'soft measures'**, including: signs, interpretation and providing information.

FOR DISCUSSION

Think about the attractions you have visited, either local or in another destination.

Have they introduced any of the visitor management techniques: control volume, modify behaviour, adapt a resource or grant's 'hard' and 'soft' measures?

4 Sustainable tourism guidelines and principles

As we have established, 'sustainable tourism' practices are of major concern, but 'best practice' and procedures are sometimes difficult to implement, as many organisations may not know how to be 'sustainable'. Therefore, some organisations have designed guidelines and principles for 'sustainable tourism implementation'.

The World Travel and Tourism Council (WTTC) ten-point guideline

1. Identify and minimise product and operational environmental problems, paying particular attention to new products.

2. Pay due regard to environmental concerns in design, planning, construction and implementation.

3. Be sensitive to conservation of environmentally protected or threatened areas, species or scenic aesthetics, achieving landscape enhancement where possible.

4. Practice energy conservation, reduce and recycle waste, practice freshwater management and control sewage disposal.

5. Control and diminish air emissions and pollutants.

6. Monitor, control and reduce noise levels.

7. Control, reduce and eliminate environmentally unfriendly products, such as asbestos, CFCs, pesticides, etc.

8. Respect and support historic or religious objects and sites.

9. Exercise due regard for the interest of local populations, including their history, traditions and culture and future developments.

10. Consider environmental issues as a key factor in the overall development of travel and tourism destinations.

Tourism Concern – ten principles of sustainable tourism

1	Using resources sustainably
2	Reducing over-consumption and waste
3	Maintaining diversity
4	Integrating tourism into planning
5	Supporting local economies
6	Involving local economies
7	Consulting stakeholders and the public
8	Training staff
9	Marketing tourism responsibly
10	Undertaking research

The Association of Independent Tour Operators (AITO) recognition

★	Employing a 'responsible tourism manager', acceptance of AITO guidelines, and provision of published advice to customers.
★★	All of the above, in addition to: performing an environmental review (audit) and company policy towards 'responsible' tourism.
★★★	All of the above two, plus: environmental initiatives in the destination.

The Association of Independent Tour Operators (AITO) responsible tourism guidelines

1	Protection of the environment – flora, fauna and landscapes
2	Respect for local cultures – traditions, religions and the built heritage
3	Economic and social benefits for local communities
4	Conservation of natural resources, from the office to the destination
5	Minimising pollution caused by noise, waste disposal and congestion

5 The World Tourism Organisation (WTO) 'Global Code of Ethics for Tourism' (GCET) (1999)

"The Global Code of Ethics for Tourism sets a frame of reference for the responsible and sustainable development of world tourism." (*Francesco Frangialli*, Secretary-General of the WTO)

Global Code of Ethics for Tourism	
1	Tourism's contribution to mutual understanding and respect between peoples and societies
2	Tourism as a vehicle for individual and collective fulfilment
3	Tourism as a factor of sustainable development
4	Tourism as a user of the cultural heritage of mankind and contributor to its enhancement
5	Tourism as a beneficial activity for host countries and communities
6	Obligations of stakeholders in tourism development
7	Rights to tourism
8	Liberty of tourists' movements
9	Rights of the workers and the entrepreneurs in the tourism industry
10	Implementation of the principles of the 'Global Code of Ethics for Tourism'

A C T I V I T Y   1   **2 0   m i n u t e s**

Research a travel, tourism or hospitality organisation of your choice, this can include: an airline, hotel or tour operator, and investigate how this organisation is performing in a 'responsible and sustainable' way, in relation to the guidelines and principles as identified in this chapter.

SUMMARY

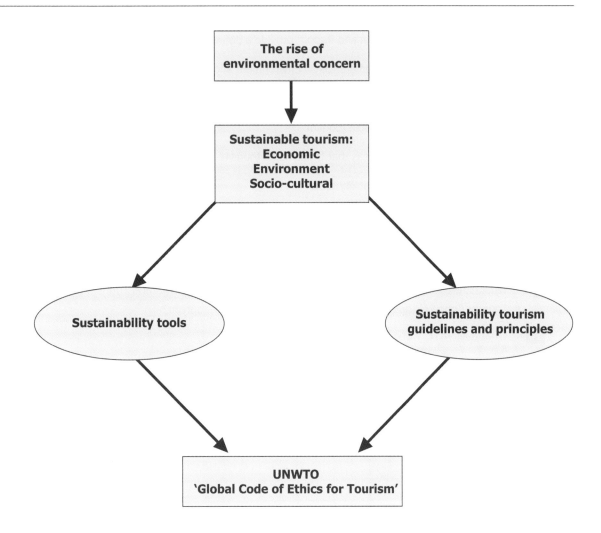

SELF-TEST QUESTIONS

1 With reference to the 'Brundtland Report' provide a definition of 'sustainable development'.

2 In what year was the UN conference on Environment and Development?

3 What is another name for this conference?

4 Give a definition of 'sustainable tourism'.

5 What are the three main areas that 'sustainable tourism' covers?

6 What are the seven sustainability tools?

7 What are the four types of carrying capacity?

8 With reference to 'visitor management', explain with examples how an attraction can better manage its visitors.

9 What differences and similarities are there between the World Travel and Tourism Council (WTTC) and Tourism Concern's guidelines and principles of sustainable tourism?

10 What does AITO stand for?

11 What is GCET an abbreviation for?

12 What is the purpose of the GCET?

SELF-TEST ANSWERS

1 'Sustainable development' can be defined as 'development that meets the needs of present without compromising the needs of future generations'.

2 The UN conference on Environment and Development was in 1992 in Rio de Janeiro, Brazil.

3 Another name for this conference is 'The Rio Earth Summit'.

4 'Sustainable tourism', can be defined as tourism that "*meets the needs of present tourists and host regions while protecting and enhancing opportunity for the future.*"

5 The three main areas that 'sustainable tourism' covers are: economic, environment and socio-cultural.

6 The seven sustainability tools are: Agenda 21, carrying capacity, corporate environmental management, environmental auditing, environmental impact assessment (EIA), environmental policies and statements and visitor management.

7 The four types of carrying capacity include: ecological, economic, perceptual and physical.

8 An attraction can better manage its visitors through restricting tourist numbers, providing leaflets and information for tourists, including education, and adapting the resource such as hardening surfaces.

9 The differences and similarities between the World Travel and Tourism Council (WTTC) and Tourism Concern's guidelines and principles of sustainable tourism, include: identify and minimise product and operational environmental problems, environmental concerns in design, planning, construction and implementation, conservation of environmentally protected or threatened areas, respect and support historic or religious objects and sites, maintaining diversity, integrating tourism into planning, and marketing tourism responsibly.

10 AITO stands for Association of Independent Tour Operators.

11 GCET is an abbreviation for Global Code of Ethics for Tourism.

12 The purpose of the GCET is to set a frame of reference for the responsible and sustainable development of world tourism.

ANSWER TO ACTIVITY

1 There is no formal answer to this activity, as the answer depend on personal research.

PRACTICE EXAMINATION

This is a real past CTH examination. Once you have completed your studies, you should attempt this under exam conditions. That means allowing yourself the full time available of 2½ hours. Do not look at the suggested answers until you have finished.

QUESTION PRACTICE

CTH Diploma courses are all assessed by examination. This method of assessment is used as it is considered to be the fairest method to ensure that students have learnt the things they have been taught.

On the following pages you will find a practice exam for this subject. When you have worked through this Study Guide and answered the self-test questions you should make a full attempt at the practice exam, preferably under exam conditions. This will give you the opportunity to practise questions in the CTH exam format.

The exam questions in this paper are examples of this subject's questions. The answers provided are notes used by the examiners when marking the exam papers. They are not complete specimen answers but are of the type and style expected. In some cases there is a list of bullet points and in others more text or essay style, however they are representative of the content expected in your responses. Information given contains the main points required by the Chief Examiner.

SECTION 1 – A1-A10 (2 mark questions)

These questions are looking for factual information and test concise and logical thinking. As a general rule, for a two mark question CTH is looking for one or two word answers or maybe a short sentence. Therefore either text or bullet points will be accepted. If two points are asked for, marks will be allocated for each point. If only one answer is asked for we would expect a short sentence.

Here we are trying to assess your knowledge of the subject and to identify if you can recall the basic principles, methods, techniques and terminology linked to the subject.

SECTION 2 – A11-A15 (4 mark questions)

These questions are looking for factual information and test concise and logical thinking. As a general rule, CTH is looking for bullet points or a short paragraph for the answer to a four mark question. If two or four points are asked for, marks will be allocated for each point. If only one answer is asked for we would expect a few sentences or a short paragraph.

Here we are trying to assess your knowledge of the subject and to identify if you understand and can demonstrate how principles, methods and techniques can be used.

SECTION 3 – B1 (20 mark questions)

These 20 mark questions are looking for factual information and how those facts can be applied to both the subject and the hospitality industry. We expect to see essay style answers to show your knowledge of the subject and its application.

From this section you need to select three questions from a choice of five. **Do not answer more than three as only the first three answers will be marked**. These are essay style questions so you should select the three that you feel you are the most prepared for. No matter how good the answer is, if it does not answer the question you will not be given any marks – marks are only allocated when the answer matches the question.

If you run out of time in the exam jot down the essential points that you intended to include; the examiner will allocate marks for any correct information given.

It is difficult to assess how much you are required to write for a 20 mark question – some people can answer in a page, other people need several pages. What is important is that you answer the question asked – it is about the quality of the answer not the quantity written.

20 mark questions

The following descriptors give you information on the CTH marking scheme and what you need to aim for at each level.

Grade	Explanation
Level 4 **(15-20)**	Demonstrates knowledge of analysis and evaluation of the subject
Level 3 **(11-15)**	Demonstrates knowledge of application of the subject
Level 2 **(6-10)**	Demonstrates knowledge and comprehension of the subject
Level 1 **(1-5)**	Does not demonstrate knowledge and understanding of the subject

Level descriptors

The following level descriptors give you information on what you need to aim for at each grade.

Grade	Explanation
Distinction	Demonstrates knowledge of analysis and evaluation of the subject
Merit	Demonstrates knowledge of application of the subject
Pass	Demonstrates knowledge and comprehension of the subject
Fail	Does not demonstrate knowledge and understanding of the subject

EXAMINATION

CTHCM Diploma in Hotel Management

Subject: **The Tourism Industry (DHM 172)**

Series: **January 2008**

Time Allowed: **2.5 hours**

Instructions:

You are allowed **TEN MINUTES** to read through this examination paper before the commencement of the examination. <u>Please read the questions carefully</u>, paying particular attention to the marks allocated to each question or part of a question, and taking account of any special instructions or requirements laid down in any of the questions.

This Examination Paper contains **TWO SECTIONS**.
Answer **ALL** questions in **Section A**.
Answer any **THREE** questions in **Section B**.

On completion of your examination:

Make sure that your name, CTHCM membership number, and centre number are clearly marked at the top of each answer sheet and on any other material you hand in.

Marks Allocation

Section A = 40% of the module grade
Section B = 60% of the module grade

SECTION A

*Answer **all** questions in this section. This section carries a total of **40** marks.*

A1.   When did mass tourism in Spain start?
      a) The 1950's
      b) The 1960's
      c) The 1970's
      d) The 1980's.   *(2 marks)*

A2.   Describe the difference between a tourist and an excursionist.   *(2 marks)*

A3.   Describe the role of VisitBritain.   *(2 marks)*

A4.   Give two examples of tourism superstructure.   *(2 marks)*

A5.   Describe the purpose and function of a tour operator.   *(2 marks)*

A6.   Explain the term serviced accommodation and give an example.   *(2 marks)*

A7.   What do the letters IATA stand for?   *(2 marks)*

A8.   Define dark tourism and give an example of such a destination.   *(2 marks)*

A9.   List the uses of transportation.   *(2 marks)*

A10.   What is meant by a fly-cruise holiday?   *(2 marks)*

A11.   Describe the role of the Civil Aviation Authority.   *(4 marks)*

A12.   List four facilitators that aid travel.   *(4 marks)*

A13.   Explain the terms allocentric and psychocentric in relation to personality
      and travel destination choice.   *(4 marks)*

A14.   List four classifications or groups of resort attractions.   *(4 marks)*

A15.   Explain the terms push factors and pull factors in relation to motivation to
      travel.   *(4 marks)*

SECTION B

Answer any __3__ questions in this section. Each question carries a total of __20__ marks.

B1.

List and discuss the factors you need to consider when planning a new tourist destination.

(20 marks)

B2.

Explain the positive economic benefits of tourism to a region or country.

(20 marks)

B3.

Explain how governments and politics influence the tourism industry from both a positive and negative perspective, giving examples to support your answer.

(20 marks)

B4.

a) Explain the term sustainable tourism.

(5 marks)

b) Discuss a range of ways in which sustainable tourism can be achieved in a tourist destination.

(15 marks)

B5.

Identify and explain possible negative socio-cultural effects of tourism that a developing country can experience when receiving large numbers of tourists from developed western countries.

(20 marks)

PRACTICE EXAMINATION
ANSWERS

SECTION A

A1   b)   The 1960s

A2   A tourist will stay at a destination for more than 24 hours and therefore requires accommodation. An excursionist stays less than 24 hours and does not require accommodation.

A3   To promote and encourage tourism to Great Britain.

A4   Hotels, shops, nightclubs, bars (any suitable example)

A5   Buys components (principally transportation and accommodation) and arranges them into a package which it offers for sale, either direct to the consumer or through a travel agent.

A6   Accommodation where services and facilities are provided to the customer in addition to the (sleeping) accommodation.

This usually means the provision of food and beverage, cleaning, laundry services and entertainment facilities such as fitness centres and nightclubs.

A7   International Air Transport Association.

A8   Visiting sites associated with death and disaster. The most visited sites associated with Dark Tourism are Ground Zero in New York, Auschwitz, Hiroshima.

A9   ▪   Travel to the destination from the tourist's place of origin and back again

   ▪   Travel around the destination

   ▪   The main feature of the trip

A10   Where a customer will fly out to, for example, Miami, board the cruise ship, take their cruise, returning to Miami and then flying home again.

A11   The CAA has four functions:

   1   The Safety Regulation Group, which is concerned with all aspects of the safe operation of air transport in the UK.

   2   The Economic Regulation Group, which regulates the airports and the airlines and advises the government on economic issues for the aviation industry.

   3   The Consumer Protection Group, which has two roles: to provide financial protection for consumers against an organiser's financial failure, which it does through the ATOL scheme, and to license airlines to make sure they comply with legislation in relation to finances, liability and insurance.

   4   The National Air Traffic Services, which is more commonly called Air Traffic Control.

A12   Four of:

   ▪   Time
   ▪   Money
   ▪   Accessibility
   ▪   Favourable exchange rates
   ▪   Visa free or visa on arrival
   ▪   Friendly locals who speak the tourist's language

A13   Allocentric personalities are outgoing, adventurous, confident, seek excitement and are keen to experiment.

   Psychocentric personalities are introverts, tend to be anxious and worriers and seek familiarity and security.

A14   Four of:

   ▪   Natural features
   ▪   Rides and transport
   ▪   Entertainment
   ▪   Sports facilities
   ▪   Shopping
   ▪   Artistic and cultural heritage

A15   The push factor involves a force which acts to drive people away from a place and the pull factor is what draws them to a new location.

   A pull factor is when something attracts you to go to that country. For example in Spain the weather is far better than the UK in the summer and will attract someone from the UK. A push factor is when something or someone makes you leave. For example: A war or hurricane would make you leave a country.

SECTION B

B1
- **Tourist attractions** – the broader the range of attractions that a destination can offer, then the more successful it is likely to be

- **Accessibility** – in terms of transportation into and around the destination

- **Investment** – is needed to develop the tourist attractions mentioned above and:

- **Superstructure and infrastructure**

- **Ease of employment** – the tourism industry is very labour intensive and therefore needs a large supply of people to service the industry

- **Favourable political climate** – both to attract potential customers and to maintain a stable tourism industry

- **Proximity to a large market** – to fulfil the demand forecasts of the industry

- **Capacity of the construction industry** – needed to build the infrastructure and superstructure mentioned above

- **A realistic and achievable development plan** – to ensure that the destination is sustainable and that the quality of the environment and the life of local residents is not disrupted

- **Availability of sites** – so that the planned tourism destination can be built

- **Local buy-in** – a fundamental principle of sustainable tourism

- **Competition** (or lack of) – if the destination can offer unique attractions, then it is (virtually) guaranteed a market, if not, it will have to compete with other destinations offering the same attractions. Less competition will mean that the destination should be more successful in attracting customers

---

B2
The impact of tourism on the economy is inevitable, but the impact can be both positive and negative. Generally, decisions by any government to implement strategy pertaining to development of its tourism potential will invariably be based on the industry's positive economic impacts. This same motivation will be exercised by public agencies at regional and local level, with commercial operators within the tourism industry also seeking to maximise their economic returns.

Tourism economic impacts can be grouped into two broad categories:

- Wealth generation
- Employment generation

Developed and developing countries are actively seeking for their tourism industry to have a positive impact on their economic activity, by means of contributing to the gross national product (GNP), creating employment opportunities and supporting the country's balance of payments.

Direct and indirect income

Income is generated from wages and salaries, interest, rent and profits. In the tourism industry, which is labour-intensive, the greatest proportion of money is likely to be derived from service commodities supplied to the tourists. The country benefits from the tourists' expenditure.

Tourism's contribution to GNP

Gross National Product (GNP) is the value of all goods and services produced by a country in a given year while Gross Domestic Product (GDP) is the amount of goods and services, measured at market prices, produced within the country during a particular time.

Period (usually a year). GDP is the amount of goods and services produced by residents of a country, regardless of where that production takes place.

A country's economic performance can be measured by analysing its gross national product; via the total value of all goods and services produced in addition to its net revenues from overseas.

The study of a tourism industry's contribution to the nation's GNP will enable the country to indicate the importance of tourism activity relative to that of other industry sectors. Countries that are dependent on tourism revenue will indicate a high figure for

Contribution to GNP and vice versa. In 1991, *Bull* identifies five major factors that determine tourism's role in GNP, and these factors that have been identified include:

- The stock resources: Natural resources, built facilities, human and financial resources are all essential prerequisites of successful tourism development.

- The state of technical knowledge: Whereby economic returns from tourism are viewed to be highest in those nations that employs high level of technical expertise.

- Social and political stability: With characteristics of heterogeneity and inseparability, tourism products do generate real or perceived problems in destination area that have detrimental effects on the number of inbound tourists as well as receipts from tourism.

- Attitudes and habits: Host/local communities views about tourism and individual tourists' tendency to travel has direct impact on the development of tourism within the destination.

- Investment: Public and private sectors' investment in capital projects and business supports such as promotion and training will influence the patterns and rates of growth of tourism development. The above mentioned factors, shows that both the demand and supply side of the tourism system have an influence over the involvement of tourism activity towards contribution of a nation's GNP.

Creation of employment

The tourism industry creates employment on a large scale in the country, as people are needed to serve the tourists. Countries that rely mainly on tourist arrivals will find that as many as 40% of the country's labour is directly or indirectly dependent on tourism for employment and income. Tourism also has ability to stimulate employment creation in sectors not directly involved in tourism activities. As such, employment created by tourism can be categorised into the following groups (World Travel and Tourism Council, 1996):

- Traditional travel service jobs: these include employments in airlines, hotels, restaurants, attractions, tour operators and travel agents.

- Government travel service jobs: such as tourism promotion and information offices, national park or monument guides, air traffic controllers, customs and immigration officials at land, air and sea borders.

- Travel and tourism capital investment jobs:
    - Public side: design and construction of highways, parks, and airports.
    - Private side: employment in conception and construction of aircraft, hotels/resorts, vacation homes, travel organisations office buildings, cruise ships, retail shops and restaurants.

- Travel product jobs: provision of goods and services to travellers and travel organisations and a range of supporting businesses that include film developers, accountants, dry cleaners, butchers, shoemakers and sign makers.

Multiplier Effect

The money spent by tourists in a country will increase exponentially as it flows back into the economy in the form of taxes, benefiting the population in terms of a better, stronger infrastructure.

Multiplier analysis is often used to estimate the current impact of tourist expenditures in a nation's economy. It is generally recognised that initial tourism expenditure will increase demand for service to satisfy tourists' needs that will filter through the economy and stimulate further indirect expenditure.

According to *Lickorish and Jenkins* (1997), tourist multipliers can be grouped into five main categories:

- Transactions or sale multipliers: whereby a rise in tourists' spending will generate additional business revenue. This usually enables a measurement in ratio between changes to be generated for analysis.

- Output multiplier: pertaining to the amount of extra output as a result of rising tourist expenditure.

- Income multiplier: measuring additional income created in the economy through the increase of tourists' spending.

- Government revenue multiplier: this measures the impact on government income from the resulting rise in tourist expenditure.

- Employment multiplier: that measures that combine employment generated by tourism development.

Balance of Payments

Balance of payments is generally deduced by government and international observers as a guide to an economy's performance. It is a statement of international flows of currency and capital items in and out of a nation. Items appearing on a country's balance of payments can be classified into:

- Visible: tangible goods such as cars, electrical products and raw materials.

- Invisible: refers to banking and insurance services, shipping and tourism.

Tourism usually plays a major role pertaining to balance of payments especially in developing nations and those that have heavy economic reliance on tourism activity. For a country's economy to be sound there has to be balance in payment. This means the funds received should balance against funds paid out. A country's economy is not sustainable if there is a marked imbalance in the buying and selling power of that country. Tourism ensures a more balanced expenditure and income in a country.

B3   Governments and politics can influence transportation which is a critical factor in the tourism industry. They can invest public money in the development of a transportation system, thereby providing access to and around the destination which are key factors in achieving a successful tourism industry.

If infrastructure and superstructure become overloaded, governments can restrict the numbers of tourists entering the area and therefore relieve pressure. This can be done by restrictions at the point of entry, most likely by visa requirements (although this would not be possible between EU member states).

In the UK, the political decisions to grant paid holiday leave and bank holidays enable people to take more holidays. Governments fund tourist offices whose function is to promote and encourage tourism to areas which has a positive influence on the tourism industry.

Governments can attract investment (both domestic and international) by the provision of tax relief and subsidies for investors.

In the UK, the political decision was taken to tender for the provision of the 2012 Olympic Games in London. As this bid has been successful, it will surely have a beneficial effect on the tourism industry in London in the years beyond 2012.

Governments and politics can, however, have a negative impact on the tourism industry. Governments and countries who have a bad political reputation or an unstable political system, such as Zimbabwe, deter the tourist from visiting, or restrictions may be imposed that makes this impossible anyway.

In political climates such as these, it is often the case that the country's currency becomes weak and unstable which does not make the destination attractive to potential tourists, indeed, it is likely to raise the cost of tourism and make the destination economically unattractive.

The governments and politicians may impose their own political views on their citizens by restricting freedom to travel to any destination that holds political views opposed to their own.

Countries operating in this type of political climate are often seen as unsafe for foreign visitors.

A government's stance on a particular issue may offend, annoy or irritate potential tourists to that country, who may choose to stay away as a political statement or protest at the government's stance.

B4 a)   The United Nations World Tourism Organisation defines sustainable tourism as tourism that meets the needs of present tourists and host regions while protecting and enhancing opportunity for the future. Rather than being a type of product, it is an ethos that underpins all tourism activities. As such, it is integral to all aspects of tourism development and management rather than being an add-on component.

The objective of sustainable tourism is to retain the economic and social advantages of tourism development while reducing or mitigating any undesirable impacts on the natural, historic, cultural or social environment. This is achieved by balancing the needs of tourists with those of the destination.

It refers to a level of tourism activity that can be maintained over the long term because it results in a net benefit for the social, economic, natural and cultural environments of the area in which it takes place.

B4 b)
- Involving the local host community in decision-making and planning for the development of tourism in the area
  - Making sure that the area does not exceed its carrying capacity by:
    - Increasing the carrying capacity (expand infrastructure and superstructure)
    - Relieving the demand pressure (open up new tourist areas and/or extend the visit season)
    - Limiting access (increase prices – which is a self regulating measure – close certain places and facilities at certain times, establish a maximum number of accommodation units, prohibit new build through zoning or permit regulations)
  - Inform, educate and encourage host and visitors alike to embrace the principals of sustainability, especially in relation to the environment by:
    - Using renewable resources
    - Using local labour and products
    - Using more environmentally-friendly forms of transportation
    - Encourage recycling
    - Paying a realistic and fair price for the tourism product used
- Planning controls
- Marketing popular attractions, not developing new ones
- Zoning strategies – one for tourists, other for visitors
- Restricted zones for further development
- Drive tourism up-market
- Traffic-free zones
- Plant trees, shrubs and install new litter bins, graffiti-free seating
- Reduce publicity and road signs to reduce possible congestion
- Introduce campaigns to create public awareness
- Rules of conduct
- Reduce numbers, attract high-spend visitors
- Attract the independent 'greener' traveller
- Provide opportunity for tourists to meet locals / keep them separated to reduce impact
- Green Flag / Green Globe Awards
- Environmental audit
- Hotels – recycling waste, using cruelty-free toiletries, control water wastage, offer the use of bicycles to guests

B5   Tourists from developed western countries will demand western amenities, have different values from that of their hosts, will almost certainly be wealthier than the host population and may well act differently as they are away from the constraints of their normal society.

The demand for western amenities will mean that local cultures and customs may well start to disappear as the area becomes 'westernised', particularly with the appearance of giant international companies.

The local population may well resent this attitude, seeing in it implied criticism that their amenities are considered inferior.

It is sometimes the case that tourism influences the younger generation more. In many areas, for example on the island of Mallorca, the young Mallorcans see tourism as a better and easier way of earning a living than the traditional way of agriculture. Thus tourism has effectively altered the traditional way of life on Mallorca as there is now insufficient numbers of younger Mallorcans to farm the land. Agriculture is now in serious decline as these young people leave the land and the homes where it is traditional for several generations of one family to live.

The different values that the western tourist may hold will include attitudes to religion, family, dress, eating and drinking. In general, these values are of more importance in the host countries and western attitudes in these areas may cause annoyance, if not outright offence to the host population.

The wealth of the visitors may lead to both resentment of the wealthy tourist and dissatisfaction with their lives within the host population. The presence of wealthy tourists may lead to an increase in both petty and serious crime.

The fact that the western tourist may act differently while away from the constraints of their normal society is linked to the points made above regarding the different value systems between hosts and visitors. The visitor's behaviour in the host country, while different from how they would normally behave at home, may again cause annoyance and offence to the host community.

BIBLIOGRAPHY

BIBLIOGRAPHY

The following key text books have been consulted in the preparation of this Study Guide, and referred to (where relevant) in the text.

Butler, RW (1980), 'The concept of the tourist area life cycle of evolution: implications for management of resources', *Canadian Geographer*, 24 (1): 5-12.

Cohen, E (2004), *Contemporary Tourism*, Elsevier, Oxford.

Cooper, C; Fletcher, J; Fyall, A; Gilbert, D; Wanhill, S (2005), *Tourism: Principles and Practice*, 3rd edition, Pearson Education Limited, Harlow, Essex.

Dale, G (2005), *Travel and Tourism* (BTEC National Book 1), Heinemann Educational Publishers, Oxford.

Dann, G (1977), 'Anomie to ego-enhancement and tourism', *Annals of Tourism Research*, 4:184-194.

De Kadt, E (1979), *Tourism: Passport to Development?*, Oxford University Press, New York.

Doxey, GV (1975), 'When enough's enough: the natives are restless in Old Niagara', *Heritage Canada 2* (2), 26-7.

Foo, J; McGuiggan, R and Yiannakis, A (2004), 'Roles tourists play: An Australian perspective', *Annals of Tourism Research*, 31 (2): 408-27.

Grant, M (1994), 'Visitor Management', *Insights*, A41-6, English Tourist Board, London.

Gray, HP (1970), *International Travel – International Trade*, Heath Lexington Books, Lexington.

Hall, CM (2000), 'Rethinking Collaboration and Partnership: A Public Policy Perspective', pp: 143-158. Tourism collaboration and partnerships, 'Politics, practice and sustainability'. Edited Bramwell, B and Lane, B, Channel View Publications.

Hall, CM & Williams, AM (2008), *Tourism and Innovation*, Taylor & Francis Ltd, Routledge.

Holloway, C (2006), *The Business of Tourism,* 7th edn., Pearson Education Limited, Harlow, Essex.

Hunziker, W & Krapf *(1941), ibid* – Burkart, A & Medlik, S (1974), *Tourism: past, present and future,* Heinemann, Oxford.

Kinnaird, V and Hall, D (Eds) (1994), *Tourism: A Gender Analysis*, Wiley, Chichester.

Lumsdon, L (1997), *Tourism Marketing*, Thomson International Business Press, London.

Moutinho, L (1987), 'Consumer behaviour in tourism', *European Journal of Marketing*, 21 (10): 3-44.

Mueller, H & EL Kaufmann (2001), 'Wellness tourism: Market analysis of a special health tourism segment and implications for the hotel industry', *Journal of Vacation Marketing*, Volume 7, No 1, p. 5.

Murray, M and Sproats, J (1990), 'The disabled traveller: Tourism and disability in Australia', *Journal of Tourism Studies*, 1 (1): 9-14.

Page, SJ and Connell, J (2006), *Tourism: A modern synthesis,* 2nd edn., Thomson Learning, London.

Pearce, DG (1989), *Tourist Development,* Harlow, Essex.

Plog, S (1974), 'Why destination areas rise and fall in popularity', *Cornell Hotel and Restaurant Administration Quarterly*, February: 55-58.

Swarbrooke, J (2002), *The Development and Management of Visitor Attractions*, 2nd edn., Butterworth-Heinemann, Oxford.

Swarbrooke, J (1999), *Sustainable Tourism Management*, CAB International, Wallingford, Oxon.

Tapper, R and Font, X (2004), 'Tourism Supply Chains', Report of a Desk Research Project for the Travel Foundation, Leeds Metropolitan University, Leeds.

INDEX